OVERPLAYED

A PARENT'S GUIDE TO SANITY
IN THE WORLD OF YOUTH SPORTS

"Every page of this book screams common sense. It's like a portable parent telling me that I'm not nuts for having questions about youth sports, and that I actually have the power to reclaim my sanity and the sanity of my entire family."

—*Scott Dannemiller, author of* The Year without a Purchase

"This is the book for parents of any kids involved in the abundance of activities our culture offers (demands of!) our kids. *Overplayed* offers biblical and developmental wisdom to enable and equip parents to buck cultural demands and instead help our children grow appropriately into the people God made them to be."

—*Caryn Rivadeneira, author of* Broke and Known and Loved

"I have been every one of the possible roles discussed in this book: professional, amateur, kid who got cut from the team, and parent of children currently in youth sports. *Overplayed* will help parents currently involved in youth sports and parents soon to begin the journey."

—*Erik Kratz, MLB catcher*

"There are so many myths associated with youth sports that we simply accept without thought or analysis as to whether they are actually true. This book is a must-read for parents as it takes a thoughtful, clear-eyed look at those myths and offers solid, helpful suggestions as to how we can, once again, make youth sports about the kids."

—*John R. Gerdy, author of* Ball or Bands

"Good parents who are questioning how sports can build Christlike character in their children will find practical suggestions within the pages of this book. The authors have done their homework in bringing to light the many challenges that confront families today. I for one am grateful that they give biblical answers as to how to navigate the sports arena in a healthy, selfless way."

—*Jim Ryun, Olympic medalist in track and field, retired U.S. representative*

"Practical and inspirational, *Overplayed* reminds and reorients us as parents and caregivers to what truly matters: not our children's scholarships, trophies, or records but the fact that they are God's beloved children."

—*Rachel S. Gerber, minister for youth and young adults for Mennonite Church USA and author, Ordinary Miracles*

"As a pastor, I have been looking for a resource on sports, faith, and families. In *Overplayed*, I have found it. The discussion questions for families and coaches in the context of sports and the church are excellent, and I plan to use it as a conversation starter with parents, youth, and coaches."

—*Ruth Boehm, pastor of Faith Mennonite Church*

OVERPLAYED

A PARENT'S GUIDE TO SANITY
IN THE WORLD OF YOUTH SPORTS

DAVID **KING** &
MARGOT **STARBUCK**

Herald Press

Harrisonburg, Virginia
Kitchener, Ontario

Library of Congress Cataloging-in-Publication Data

Names: King, David, 1953-
Title: Overplayed : a parent's guide to sanity in the world of youth sports /
    David King & Margot Starbuck.
Description: Harrisonburg : Herald Press, 2016. | Includes bibliographical
    references.
Identifiers: LCCN 2015037464 | ISBN 9780836199727 (pbk. : alk. paper)
Subjects: LCSH: Parenting—Religious aspects—Christianity. | Child
    rearing—Religious aspects—Christianity. | Sports—Religious aspects
    —Christianity.
Classification: LCC BV4529 .K557 2016 | DDC 248.8/45--dc23 LC record
available at http://lccn.loc.gov/2015037464

OVERPLAYED
© 2016 by Herald Press, Harrisonburg, Virginia 22802
    Released simultaneously in Canada by Herald Press,
    Kitchener, Ontario N2G 3R1. All rights reserved.
Library of Congress Control Number: 2015037464
International Standard Book Number: 978-0-8361-9047-5
Printed in United States of America
Cover and interior design by Merrill Miller
Photo of sky by Janni Wet/iStockphoto/Thinkstock

To order or request information, please call 1-800-245-7894 or visit
www.heraldpress.com.

20 19 18 17 16   10 9 8 7 6 5 4 3 2 1

To Deb, Derek, Ryan, and Lisa: my favorite team.
—Dave

For my three little athletes: may you always enjoy the game.
—Margot

Contents

Introduction

Why This Book?

I (Dave) have been accused of biting the hand that feeds me.

Athletics directors aren't supposed to speak out about the perils of sports.

Having worked for thirty-four years in coaching and athletics—at the elementary, middle school, high school, and university levels—I'm committed to the physical, social, and emotional benefits of sport. For the last decade I have worked as director of athletics at a Christian university in Virginia. Sports have been a huge part of not only my professional life but also my family's life. I played soccer, basketball, and baseball in college, and my wife, Deb, played volleyball. Our three kids, now young adults, have played volleyball, basketball, and field hockey.

During my almost thirty-five years in sports and education, however, I have seen the landscape of youth sports change dramatically. And like many parents I speak with, I've become increasingly concerned about the toll that current youth sports culture is taking on children, young people, and families. Families' dollars and time are stretched and stressed. Children are suffering overuse injuries and burning out at younger and younger ages. They're being asked to perform beyond appropriate developmental stages. They're failing to develop some of the intrinsic values that adults *assume* sports will teach them. Parents are damaging their relationships with their kids and with each other. And far too often, as we struggle to navigate this new terrain, we're driven not by love but by fear.

About ten years ago I set out on a journey of studying, reading, and listening to understand what I was observing. I read nearly all the mainstream books that have been written about the challenges of youth sports and whether parents are serving their children well by overcommitting them at younger and younger ages. The book I wanted to read would help families reflect on how their children's athletic involvements are or are not forming them into kingdom people. The book would empower parents to make great choices about balancing their kids' athletic pursuits with other commitments to family, church, and community.

I couldn't find that book.

So with the encouragement of many people, I began putting my ideas on paper. I soon realized, however, that an aging athletics director—who didn't play a lot of youth sports when he was young (they didn't exist!) and whose kids were well past the youth sports age—would do well to team up with someone "in the trenches." I needed the perspective of a parent navigating the world of youth sports, someone who would both support and challenge my ideas and add relevant stories of her own. I found that person in Margot Starbuck.

I (Margot) also care deeply about equipping families to live well as God's people in the world. While Dave's family is no longer in the stage of carting kids around to practices and games, mine is smack-dab in the middle of it. Having competed in basketball and track in high school, and having coached Special Olympics basketball in California for five years, I am now parenting three teens who play volleyball, basketball, soccer, and baseball. As a speaker, writer, and mother, I have written books and articles and given lots of talks about what God intends for our bodies and about loving our neighbors. I see the field, the court, the track, the diamond, and the ice as great places to explore these ideas further.

The most relevant credentials aren't our successes; they're our failures. Before my son Rollie could speak, he could pantomime motions for basketball, football, and baseball. He was magic with any ball he touched. When his language developed later than most, I convinced myself it was because his physical skills were so hyperdeveloped. (This logic relieved my anxiety.) For years, he was *that* kid: the one who excelled at every sport. But as I was working on this book, Rollie made the decision *not* to try out for his school's soccer team as a ninth grader. And even though it was the right choice for Rollie, I am grieving a little bit.

Like Margot, I (Dave) have also had to catch myself a few times. When my son Ryan began playing basketball at a junior college in Kansas and folks would inquire about how he was doing, I'd respond, "Yes, he's at Hesston College, but he isn't playing very much." The third time I spoke it, I finally *heard* what I was communicating: *in order to be successful, he had to be the star who got a lot of playing time.* And yet being selected to play college ball had already put him ahead of 95 percent of the guys who'd played in high school the year before. That observation was a good gut check to remind me that we're all capable of irrational thoughts and behaviors when our children are involved.

So we both understand the temptations and pressures—which don't always even rise to consciousness!—facing parents of young athletes. We've been there.

WHY NOW?

Ultimately, we both love sports. We love our kids and other people's kids. We love God. We've got a lot of questions about the direction and demands of the youth sports movement today. The fact that you picked up this book means that you're asking questions too.

So we want you to know: you're not alone.

Lots of parents are asking the same questions we are because childhood has changed radically in recent decades. In our fast-paced world, with a plethora of opportunities for families, parents and kids are often moving at a hectic pace. Only 57 percent of families are having dinner together five nights a week. Kids witness the mad scramble between parents to coordinate schedules, and they keenly discern the undercurrent of pressure to succeed. Some families that are already stretched thin—two parents working, commitments at church, Suzuki instrument lessons, advanced placement courses in middle school, academic clubs, community involvement—are adding various levels of youth sports to their lives. Unfortunately, the success-oriented nature of youth sports, like so many other areas of our children's lives, only adds more pressure to a child's already confusing world.

With the best of intentions, parents line the bleachers on Saturday mornings and holler their support at each game. And yet, in his letter to parents of the Little League team he was coaching, Mike Matheny, former Major League Baseball player and manager of the St. Louis Cardinals, observes, "I believe that . . . loud cheering and 'Come on, let's go, you can do it' . . . just adds more pressure to the kids. . . . You as parents need to be the silent, constant source of support." If Matheny is right about the unintended results of cheering—which we suspect he is—then there are likely other things parents of young athletes do that communicate messages we do not intend.

In these pages we'll explore practical questions like this one, as well as deeper questions about how our families can live faithfully. We'll examine the ways in which our decisions are, at times, moved by fear instead of love. We want to equip adults to navigate the current landscape of youth sports in the way that best serves children.

WHAT DOES FAITH HAVE TO DO WITH YOUTH SPORTS?

In addition to offering practical tips, we want to inspire families to live daily from their foundational values. We're convinced that sports provide some of the richest experiences in which we can learn about ourselves, other people, and God, and what happens when those three intersect. Sports themselves are neither good nor bad. It is up to us to decide whether we'll use sports or be used by them.

We believe that in all arenas of life—wherever we give our thoughts, time, money, and energy—Christians are charged to engage thoughtfully and purposefully. As we've considered what this means for families navigating choices around youth sports, one particular challenge from the apostle Paul—who reportedly never once paid an athletic fee or visited a concession stand—has inspired us: "Do not conform to the pattern of this world, but be transformed by the renewing of your mind. Then you will be able to test and approve what God's will is— his good, pleasing and perfect will" (Romans 12:2).

The "pattern of this world"—those messages that we hear daily and that reinforce the world's values—roar loudly in the ears of parents:

> *You owe your child every opportunity to excel.*
> *Everyone else is doing it.*
> *He'll be left behind.*

Bullied by the world's values, we're driven by fear.

We're convinced, though, that the voice we're invited to follow speaks more gently to our hearts:

> *Love one another.*
> *Grow in wisdom, stature, and in favor with God and others.*
> *Whoever wants to become great among you must be your*
>   *servant, and whoever wants to be first must be slave of all.*

Don't worry: we're not suggesting that your kid should slack off on defense or kick the soccer ball into an opponent's goal! We're saying that followers of Christ will sometimes make choices that are different from the ones those around us are making. We want to support you in those decisions.

WHY THIS STYLE?

We've organized this book around the most popular myths of youth sports today—ideas that have circulated for so long and with such frequency that many of us don't question them. Some parents have believed one or more of these myths because our child's volunteer coach said they were true. Or perhaps even because our nine-year-old insisted they were true. In these pages we want to help you discern between what's false—"If my child doesn't start soccer at age three, she won't be good enough to play for her high school"—and what's true—"Three-year-olds haven't yet developed the spatial awareness to master the skills required to play soccer well"; "Every child develops differently"; "One young soccer player peaks at ten and is passed by a late bloomer who worked hard at age twelve."

More importantly, as people of faith we want to give you tools to discern between what might be *factually* true—"The coach at my child's high school will recruit players who've been playing in our local elite league"—from what is *ultimately* true—"The most important thing in the holistic development of my child's body, mind, soul, and spirit is not whether she plays for her high school's lacrosse team." Like you, we see the long game. We care who children will be when they're thirty, forty, and fifty years old. Because we care about raising children to be who God created them to be, we want to offer tools to help you do that.

That said, the myths and realities we're unpacking apply to parents of all faiths or no faith. But people who follow Christ do bring particular resources to the table when we consider making choices that are different from the culture around us.

WHY IS IT FOR YOU?

Each time we share our concerns about youth sports culture with an audience, one parent will typically corner us in the hallway, whispering, "Thank you! I thought I was the only one."

He's not.

She's not.

And you're not.

A lot of us are identifying some real problems with the culture of organized youth sports today. But here's the good news: you—parents, grandparents, coaches, pastors, and educators—are the solution.

You might be the solution in small ways: just by checking in with your child on the ride home from the game rather than weighing in with your opinion. Or you might be the solution in big ways: by organizing a team or league that's fun and educational and strengthens children. In big ways and small ones, we're confident that you have what it takes to equip your child, and others, to have a great experience in youth sports. As an adult, you have the capacity to see how youth sports fit into the rest of life. You have the ability to make decisions that help your children reach those long-term goals for a meaningful life, not just the short-term ones for success at a sport.

And we realize that every parent approaches sports differently. You might be that parent who is gunning to sign your two-year-old up for toddler T-ball. You might be the one who dreads the day when your nine-year-old begs you to play travel ball. You may even be the ambivalent parent of a high school athlete who is already feeling burned out. Whether reluctant or eager, a parent of younger or older kids, you are the key to your child having a fun, positive experience of sports.

We've stood in your grass-stained shoes, and we believe that real relief is available for active families and kids today.

THE POTENTIAL OF YOUTH SPORTS

I (Dave) can trace my passion for the potential of youth sports to shape a life back to a single day in seventh grade.

As was her standard routine, my math teacher placed the test facedown on my desk. I slowly peeled the test off my desk, and my eyes caught a big red F in the upper right-hand corner. I stealthily slid it into my notebook, and no one ever knew about my math fail.

Later that afternoon, in a middle school basketball game, I encountered quite a different experience. Our team was losing

You're not alone

Does it feel like you're the only parent asking some of these hard questions about youth sports? Trust us: you're not. Lots of others are silently wondering the same things you are. We encourage you to get the conversation started. Here are some ideas for doing so.

A. Very easy

Start the conversation on social media.
- How has a travel team benefited your child or family?
- How has a travel team been a challenge for your child or family?
- Have you ever said no to a sports experience for your child? What happened?

B. Not hard

Work with another parent at church to schedule one Sunday school hour where families can start this conversation. See our discussion guide at www.heraldpress.com/overplayed

C. Takes some energy and effort

Create a league, or even a single team, of kids from church and school who want to play for fun and skill development. Schedule a scrimmage against another team, or send out an email to other parents inviting their kids to a pickup game at a local park.

by two points. As I took a shot with only a few seconds remaining in the game, I was fouled. The ball didn't go in, but I got two foul shots. I calmly went to the foul line . . . and promptly missed both shots. Unfortunately, I didn't have a notebook in which to hide *that* test!

Only later would I see how deeply formative sports had been in my development, and I also saw that they could be in the lives of others. During my senior year of high school, as I was considering what I wanted to do with my life after graduation, I realized that I'd learned more about my own personhood on the court, the field, and the diamond than I had learned in Sunday school. (I say this with great respect for the men and women who taught me in Sunday school!) I learned from noticing my responses when I failed in public. I learned how to respond when the coach didn't play me. I learned from consequences when I hadn't conditioned properly. I began to understand that sports were my avenue for learning lessons for life. For other kids it was photography or theater, writing or computers, music or art. But for me, athletics provided the opportunity to become the person I wanted to be. The day I got an F and missed my foul shots guided my decision to help children, teens, and young adults have a great experience of sports.

So I don't see my critique of youth sports as "biting the hand that feeds me." Nor am I suggesting that we're all winners and everyone deserves a trophy. I'm committed to excellence, to equipping young people with skills, and to encouraging them to work hard to improve and contribute to the team. But these things have to be done at the right time and in ways that are congruent with the developmental stages of kids.

Youth sports also carry great potential for helping us view our bodies in healthy ways. Perhaps because I (Margot) had a sporty older brother, athletics were a big part of my childhood:

swimming, skateboarding, roller skating, ice-skating, skiing, baseball, softball, basketball, track, and deck tennis. (Google it. Deck tennis was very big at Camp Miniwanca in the 1980s.) In 1979 I was one of two girls in the Glen Ellyn Baseball League. And while my teammates blamed me for our purple jerseys—I really did love purple—I maintain to this day that I had nothing to do with the jerseys. Go Owls!

The Women's Sports Foundation reports that girls who play sports in high school are more likely to get good grades in school, are more likely to graduate, and are more likely to avoid an unintended pregnancy, have higher levels of confidence, have higher levels of self-esteem, and have a more positive body image. Every one of those proved true in my experience as a young female athlete.

Because so many women, young and old, do suffer from negative body image, I wrote a book called *Unsqueezed* about God's good intentions in giving us bodies that are *instrumental,* made to love God and others, and not just *ornamental,* made to be consumed by the eyes of others. Though I'm the first person to hang some stylish ornaments on my body—jazzy lime-green earrings, a sparkly nose stud, a colorful Ugandan paper bead necklace—I understand that my body is fundamentally made for movement and for relationship. And while it's not particularly quantifiable, I believe that I came to know my body as good because of the opportunities I had to play sports as a girl.

In these pages, we are advocating for kids to have great experiences of sports like the ones that so positively shaped our own lives. It's where God has met us, and we believe it's where God can meet your child and your family. In these pages we will talk with parents, pastors, and coaches about the peril and promise of children's sports. We will learn practical ways to set boundaries and help kids gain healthy identities as beloved children of God—both on and off the field, and whether they win or lose.

Myth One

Because We Owe Our Children Every Opportunity, We Can't Say No to Youth Sports

When Jennifer's son, Justin, was two years old, she opened his blue canvas tote bag after daycare to find a registration form for Soccer Stars. Soccer Stars' glitzy website assured parents like Jennifer that the company was the leader in youth soccer development for children ages two through five. The program, offered at the daycare each Friday morning for eight weeks, would add $160, over two months, to the cost of daycare.

Concerned about finances and unconvinced Justin needed to be developing anything beyond basic life skills at age two, Jennifer and her husband, Ed, agreed that their son could probably live without Soccer Stars.

Because the first week of Soccer Stars was free, Justin came home with a sticker on his back instructing his parents: "Enroll me soon. I did Soccer Stars!"

Jennifer and Ed didn't enroll him.

The next Friday, only the children whose parents had registered them played soccer. Of the fifteen students in the classroom, fourteen had paid. During the only outside time in the day, Justin stayed inside, alone. Wanting her son to enjoy beautiful fall days and play with his friends, Jennifer reluctantly signed him up.

Two years later, when Justin was four, Jennifer and some of the other preschool moms were enjoying lunch together at an Italian restaurant, commiserating about the way that their babies were growing up. It was kindergarten registration season, and the women were discussing whether their children would go in the fall.

The conversation—about what was in the very best interest of their children—kept circling back to sports. Not elementary school sports, but *high school* sports. Several moms were figuring out the relation between their children's birthdays and the registration dates for the local youth sports programs. One of them remembered reading that the "most successful" ten-year-old ice hockey players had birthdays between September and December. When they registered as ten-year-olds, they were a full nine to eleven months older than those whose birthdays were in June, July, and August. As parents of young children, these moms knew what a difference nine months can make in physical and emotional development. "Redshirting" their five-year-olds—postponing kindergarten for one year—meant that they would be bigger, faster, and stronger when it was time for them to play high school sports.

Jennifer was unwilling to join the crowd, and Justin began kindergarten in the fall.

As Justin moved into his elementary years, Ed and a friend of his, another dad, coached Justin's soccer team for their town's parks and recreation department. The team practiced Tuesday nights at six o'clock and played a game every Saturday morning. Both coaches agreed that, win or lose, their aim was to give the kids some exercise, teach them a few skills, and set them free to have fun.

On Saturdays in the bleachers, though, Jennifer began to hear anxious conversations between families. Tryouts were coming up for a local elite soccer club. Though Jennifer wasn't yet convinced that "elite" was a good descriptor for a class of humans who still couldn't get all their urine in the toilet, she listened in.

"I don't really want to pay four hundred and fifty dollars or drive to practices three nights a week or travel to tournaments on weekends," Jennifer's friend Amy bemoaned. "But I feel like I *owe* it to him."

And there it was.

Amy had spoken aloud what the nagging, niggling little voice had been hissing in Jennifer's ear:

You owe it to him.

He deserves it.

All the other kids are doing it.

Other parents are willing to sacrifice for their children to play.

Don't be selfish.

If you care about him . . .

In Jennifer's best moments, when she looked out the kitchen window to see Justin playing—"carving" a stick with a butter knife, playing hide-and-seek with a neighbor, or having a competition to see who could kick the ball over the roof of the garage—a quiet, sane voice assured her that he was already doing what young boys are meant to do.

But in other moments, that other voice—the one that insisted she was failing him because she wasn't signing him up for elite sports—was pretty persuasive. And that pressure to "keep up with the Smiths" created a knot in her stomach that stayed with her.

TIMES HAVE CHANGED SINCE YOU WERE A KID

The number of children between the ages of six and seventeen involved in youth sports today is about 21.5 million, according to one estimate. That's a lot of kids.

Today parents feel the pressure—sometimes more than our kids do!—to sign up for whatever will give children the greatest chance to be successful in sports and to keep up with others. The messages from travel team coaches, entrepreneurs, club directors, and other parents are often persuasive: Start young. Specialize early. Develop skills. Condition. Find the right travel team.

But experts in the fields of sports and medicine are telling a different story. According to one report, college coaches, scientists, physicians, and psychologists—professionals who have studied children and physical activity for years—are warning that "extreme, early focus on one sport [is] a problematic approach to developing youth athletes."

Without ever asking why, we are subjecting our kids to systems that we don't fully understand and ones that may actually harm them. In the beginning we might register our children for sports with no higher expectations than that they'll get a little exercise and have fun with friends. Then we might bump them up a league to help them get the kind of "skill development" that will help them succeed against more competitive players. Before we know it, we can't remember the last weekend our family spent in the same city or one that cost us less than $400. We find ourselves stretched physically, financially, and emotionally. And we wonder how we ended up like this.

The question Jennifer faced at every stage of her child's development still stands: Do you owe your child the experience of playing increasingly competitive youth sports?

Those who know us know our answer: No, you do not.

THE BIG PICTURE

We don't believe that any parent "owes" this to her child. But Christian parents, in particular, are guided by a set of values that equips us to offer a child a loving yes, at times, and a loving no, at other times. Just as there's no one-size-fits-all

Questions to ask ourselves

We can evaluate athletic opportunities through the lens of our commitment to Christ. Helpful questions to reflect on include:

- Are we loving God and our neighbors? (Matthew 22:37-39)
- Are we, like Jesus, growing in wisdom and in stature and in favor with God and others? (Luke 2:52)
- Are we being conformed to the pattern of this world rather than transformed by the renewing of our minds? (Romans 12:2)
- Are we being faithful stewards of our resources? (1 Corinthians 4:2)
- Are we living a sacrificial life of love patterned after Jesus? (Luke 9:24)

choice for families to make about youth sports, nor is there a spiritual formula to figure it out! But we want you to hear that you already have tools in your toolbox to help you navigate these choices.

We also encourage you to start this conversation with other parents at your church. Some may choose to do a discussion series during Christian education hour at church. Others may choose to host a single Saturday morning breakfast discussion in your neighborhood or at your church. (Find study guides at www.heraldpress.com/overplayed). We've found that some of the best resources to help Christian parents navigate youth sports are other Christian parents.

As a parent, you can see a bigger picture than your child sees. You do not owe it to your child to get caught up in a league whose functional philosophy is "select the best and leave the rest." You do not owe a child a slot in a system that eliminates more than it retains. In this system, children who don't yet excel are not selected. Then they're right back where they started: without opportunity for physical exercise and play with others. Those who are selected are given messages about their abilities that may or may not be true when it comes to their potential to play high school or college sports.

Participating in youth sports has clear benefits, but it can be difficult to find a healthy balance. For most families, the decision isn't a simple one. Some may have a child who could really thrive in a more rigorous sports environment. Other children will flourish in a more relaxed program. In good conscience, you might also decline entirely the significant time, money, and expectations that organized sports require. The best option facing parents in this situation is not always clear, and a community of faith can help us discern both our guiding values and how they apply in specific situations.

COSTS OF YOUTH SPORTS: OBVIOUS AND HIDDEN

As your family considers how to navigate the opportunities available during your child's childhood, consider some of the real costs of competitive youth sports, particularly any involvement beyond the local, recreational level.

Money

It ain't cheap.

Former Cincinnati Bengals kicker Travis Dorsch is now an assistant professor at Utah State University. He calculates that some families making $50,000 annually are spending as much as 10.5 percent of their gross income on youth athletics.

Michael Sagas is on staff at the University of Florida. During his daughter's most recent season of travel soccer, he calculated the total cost to be $18,115.41.

These might seem like extreme cases. But if you are just getting into the youth sports scene, it's important for you to know that the registration cost for the local recreation league can vary anywhere from $100 to $400. This varies greatly depending on the sport. As you move "up" to travel, elite, select, or premier teams, the costs also rise, with the low end for a season being $500 and the high end being $2,000. Those figures don't even include the costs for equipment, travel, meals, lodging, and sometimes entry fees for weekend tournaments.

While that's a choice some households can make, others cannot. One out of five disadvantaged households doesn't have children playing youth sports because of the cost. We lament the fact that the term *elite* refers not only to a specific level of team play (supposedly related to athletic ability) but also to the upper middle class who can afford it.

And even if your family can afford to play, or is willing to go into debt to do it, that doesn't necessarily mean that you should.

Time

If we're willing, it's possible to count the dollars we'll spend on youth sports. But who has time to count the time? For Christian families, does the way we spend our time reflect the priorities with which we've been commissioned: loving God and loving people? If our commitments to our faith communities and neighbors and those in need have been marginalized by athletic commitments, it may be time to reexamine the way we're using our time.

Don Schumacher is the executive director of the National Association of Sports Commissions. He reports that although fewer young people are participating in team sports every year—something we'll explore in this book—the people who are participating "are participating with a vengeance. They are playing a lot of games and entering a lot of tournaments."

Those games and tournaments often include several weekly practices, games on weekends, and travel to other in-state or out-of-state cities for competitions. When these obligations conflict with other family commitments—going to Grandma's ninetieth birthday party or volunteering at vacation Bible school—parents often have to choose between two good things. We believe it's legitimate for parents to make decisions, based on their values and family priorities, that won't be popular with coaches and, sometimes, their own children. Choosing to make these decisions together, on the day the coach hands out the schedule, can cut down on stress and anxiety as the season progresses.

The claim that competitive youth sports require a heavy investment of time isn't a judgment. It's a reality. If you believe you have to attend every one of your children's games—more on this later—the amount of time your family gives to sports increases even more.

We understand that, for some families, it works out. We know families who, willing to invest the money and hours and days, like to pack up the cooler and have a weekend adventure. Like most parents, we know that "car time" is when some of the best conversations with our kids can happen. But we also know other families who have weighed the investment of time and have decided to spend theirs in other ways. We want you to hear that even though it might seem like a countercultural choice, that's a legitimate option.

Time is a precious resource, and we all have a limited supply. As parents, we need to be good stewards of our family's time and model good choices for our children.

Physical risk

In 2014, 1.35 million children suffered sports-related injuries severe enough to send them to hospital emergency departments. One in every five kids who go to emergency rooms for treatment is there for sports injuries. While many of those injuries are the natural consequence of children being active, more and more are recognized as overuse injuries. Nearly half of all injuries to middle school and high school students are overuse injuries.

There is also a pyramid of sorts with regard to injury prevention and treatment. Knowledge of how to prevent injuries, let alone how to treat them, is virtually nonexistent in youth sports. Many coaches are not even required to have first aid certification. Injury prevention and care are slowly introduced as the competitive level rises, however, to the extent that we have personal trainers and medical personnel in abundance at major university and professional levels. What would it be like if we put more resources into injury prevention and treatment at the earliest ages?

While the physical risk of youth sports is normally identified by injury rate statistics, a child's general health condition can actually decline as well. Skipped family mealtime, an abundance of fast food and late-night snacks, and inactivity associated with playing more games than practices: these can all lead to unhealthy lifestyles for children. On the flip side, the increasingly competitive nature of youth sports means that many children who need to be physically active but who won't make the cut to play for competitive leagues are falling through the cracks.

In fact, during the past thirty years—the period in which youth sports have exploded—the obesity rate among children has doubled. That's a paradox that our culture has yet to grasp.

Emotional risk

Okay, okay. "Emotional risk" sounds like what you'd consider after a bad breakup if you were thinking about dating again. What we're describing for children involved in sports, though, is the kind of emotional experience they'll have in relation to coaches. And parents.

A three-year study of young adults' childhood experiences of organized sports, conducted in the United Kingdom, revealed that 75 percent of respondents reported some type of psychological harm from the sport. This included feeling undermined or diminished by coaches or other players.

In the United States, 70 percent of children who begin a sport by the age of eight drop out of it by the time they're thirteen years old. Behind that statistic are too many kids who've lost their love for the sport and their enjoyment of play.

It breaks our hearts to see the damaged relationships between parents and children when parents push a child beyond what she wants to do. It is hard to listen to a parent bark criticism at a child for the way he plays. (Think about it: criticizing a child for the way she plays makes no more sense than shaming a child for building a faulty sand castle. But we parents sometimes lose our good judgment when sports are involved.)

Also, because youth sports are often organized according to adult ideas of how things should be done, children are exposed to concepts and experiences before they are developmentally ready. This can cause emotional scars. For example, the number one reason children give for playing is to have fun. If concepts of competition, winning, or playing time based on performance are introduced too early, they can harm a child's sense of identity and relationships.

Loss of age-appropriate play

When was the last time you accidentally dropped a Frisbee onto the neighbor's German Shepherd after chucking a basketball at it to free it from a tree?

Pressed by responsibilities, adults often have a difficult time remembering what it was like to be a child. So when we organize sports for kids, what we create is often marked by "adult" priorities. Full-length fields, ten-foot baskets, uniforms the major athletes are wearing, prominent scoreboards and up-to-the-minute standings: these have become standard for youth sports programs. Some parents unable to attend children's games are even tracking along from their work cubicles on apps that provide live stats!

Often, however, our children haven't developed the cognitive or physical skills required to thrive under the mantle of those standards. Rather, kids are best served when adults who design athletic competitions recognize and honor children's natural stages of development: spatial awareness, competitive drive, emerging personal identity, and ability to build relationships.

Bob Bigelow, a former NBA player who lectures on how to restore a healthier perspective on youth sports, concludes that before the age of twelve, children can't understand their role in team sports. They're just too young. Bigelow makes a few more claims as well, based on his research. He suggests that "for youth sports programs to be effective, the age-appropriate needs of children must be met."

And don't miss what Bigelow says next. He writes, "There is absolutely no correlation between athletic development in children and their potential for athletic success in high school and beyond." That's pretty instructional! We're thinking especially of the explosion in the number of elite travel teams in many communities, as well as the frantic drive of many parents who push their kids to excel in sports in pursuit of college scholarship monies—which may or may not actually exist. (We'll dig into this more in chapter 7.)

We promise you: no college coach has ever recruited a player because his team won the Maple Grove Invitational U12 baseball showcase. Not only is it possible that the most gifted seven-year-old player might not continue to develop into a strong player, but the chances are also high that that child will drop out due to either burnout or overuse injury. It is just as possible that some other child, a late bloomer, will surpass the gifted seven-year-old when they both get to high school.

There is simply no evidence that success in the younger years translates into success in high school, college, or professional sports.

Relational costs and benefits

Depending on your age, you may remember playing kick the can in the street while adults in your neighborhood sat on porches and chatted with one another. Maybe the kids on your street organized pickup games of kickball or baseball. Many families today, though, report that children aren't even *in* their neighborhoods. They're at piano lessons, city chorus, French tutoring, or a session with a professional trainer.

Those committed to higher and higher levels of youth sports are extracted, in many ways, from the life of their communities. Joining extended family for vacation becomes more difficult. Time for free play in the neighborhood is reduced. Opportunities for kids to build relationships with other children, adults, volunteers, and staff at church are compromised. Attending a cousin's weekend wedding becomes unwieldy.

Despite the drawbacks, many families, especially those committed to living out their faith in the world, choose to invest in the relationships they develop through youth sports. They'll share rides to practice and games. They'll bring food and drink for other families. They'll rally to care for the family on the team who has lost a loved one. They'll invite another family to join them one week at church. When Christian families do choose sports commitments, the bleachers become the place where they seize opportunities to love God and others.

As you consider the kinds of sports opportunities you do or don't "owe" your child, we encourage you to weigh the money, time, physical risk, emotional risk, efficacy of early involvement, and relational implications. Ideally, you will consider these things *before* making the decisions that will shape the way your child experiences his or her childhood. We believe you can do this well because choices about your family's involvement in youth sports aren't made in a vacuum: they're informed by the values you already hold.

IS IT LOVE?

We also want to note that the little voice in our heads that says we "owe" it to our children—giving them an extra edge over others, or at least helping them not fall behind—can often mask itself as the voice of love.

"If you love your child, then you'll do everything you can to..."

The myth sometimes finds traction in the stories of industrious Depression-era grandparents or great-grandparents, who worked their fingers to the bone to provide for their families. Of a kindly aunt who sacrificed the pork chop so that a nephew could eat. Of the dad who took on an early-morning paper route to contribute to the family's well-being. These were loving adults who wanted their children to do better than they did. They sacrificed so that their children could survive and thrive.

Those are some solid values.

But for many middle-class families today, this is not that day.

More often, for us, the hissing voice insisting that we "owe" our children a particular athletic experience—four consecutive seasons of a sport annually, an elite travel team, a personal trainer—isn't derived from the same place. Though we convince ourselves that "giving our children everything we can" is predicated on love, more often it is built on fear.

Janine is the mother of a teenage dancer. She recognizes this pulsing anxiety in her parent peers in sports and also in education. "So many people are in such a panic that their kid won't have a shot at life if they don't get into the right school or right team or right training program," she reflects. "I see a lot of people who are completely freaked out about ensuring that their children have access to the kind of professional lives they have, and they're going to invest any sum in tutors, enrichment, elite sports, and more to make sure."

That's not love. That's fear.

BUT THEY'LL BE SHUT OUT

Many parents believe, "If my child doesn't play in this particular program, he or she won't make the high school team." Unfortunately, this type of language is being used more frequently as the politics of youth sports rears its ugly head.

That may be true. It may not.

John Amaechi, once a starting center for the Cleveland Cavaliers, did not pick up a basketball until he was seventeen years old. He didn't play organized youth basketball, and he did okay.

Todd Phillips, the first and only All-American men's basketball player at Eastern Mennonite University, where I (Dave) work, never played AAU basketball. (AAU, or the Amateur Athletic Union, is an American organization that sponsors programs in a variety of sports and offers tournaments for these local clubs.) And Todd did okay.

But let's say your child isn't John Amacchi or Todd Phillips. Where you live, it might actually be *true* that if your child doesn't play for a particular club, or in a particular league, or by a particular age, he won't have the opportunity to play for his high school team.

Would that be the end of the world? Do you want to be a part of that politicized system?

If you make decisions that align with your family's values and mission—which might include dinners together as a family, or time with your church community on Sundays—you have won. Having your child move on to the next level of local or regional athletics really isn't worth sacrificing what matters most.

As you consider whether you "owe" it to your child, weigh whether the "it" under consideration is the ultimate "it." Weigh whether you'd like to offer your child a different experience.

BUT THEY LOVE IT

In some cases, parents are the ones pushing to increase a child's involvement in sports. In other cases, children are doing the pushing. In others, it is the coach.

When I (Dave) speak to clubs, organizations, and churches about the realities of youth sports today, someone in the audience, during Q&A or later over coffee, will usually comment, "You know, it's really difficult, because our kids really enjoy it. They really want to do it."

If I'm in a good mood, I'll listen politely.

If I'm not, I'll go old school on 'em.

"Well," I'll offer, "When my son Ryan was little, he often wanted to eat a whole carton of ice cream. But I didn't let him. I knew that too much of a good thing meant he'd be less likely to enjoy it later."

I say it with a smile. But they get the message.

We know what's good for our kids and what's not. Somehow, when it comes to sports, we lose our good parenting sense. It starts innocently enough, but before you know it, you're like the family we know who suddenly realized their son was playing on four baseball teams. During the same season! Parents with the best of intentions pick up their kids from soccer practice at school, grab a Big Mac on the way to club practice, and then stop on the way home for open gym for the basketball team.

And statistics are showing that we're not doing our kids any good by losing our voices when it's time to say no. Kids who have played hard at young ages are burning out by ages thirteen and fourteen. By the time they get to college—the era in which many parents hope their children will peak in terms of athletics—they have dropped out of the sport altogether. It is certainly a phenomenon that surprised me (Dave) when I became a college athletics director, and it's a phenomenon to which we need to pay attention.

There's a time to say yes to playing a sport five days a week. There's a time to say yes to traveling three hours to play in a tournament. There's a time to invest money into a young person's athletic improvement. But when we say yes at the wrong time, or to a child who'd benefit from a no, we increase the likelihood that our children will drop out of sports early, suffer from overuse injuries, and miss out on other aspects of childhood.

DO I OWE IT?

The question remains. Do you owe it to your child to register him or her for a team every time one is offered?

Is it your parental obligation to give your kid a leg up—or a shin guard up—on other kids?

No. It's never your obligation.

But we do recognize that seizing opportunities for advancement might be exactly the right thing for your child. As your

What does our family value?

In the hustle and bustle of family life, we aren't always purposeful about articulating what we value. Here are a few questions to help your family identify your "family values." (Note: These don't need to be specific to sports. In fact, it's better if they aren't. After you have a good discussion, *then* you can figure out how to apply them to different areas of family life.)

- What do we want to be doing with our money?
- What do we want to be doing with our time?
- What relationships are most important for us to honor?
- What are three to five values we want to name as being important to us?

TIP: Identifying your family's values in advance gives you tools for decision making about athletic commitments and other types of activities.

family life unfolds, it may be that you discover your son lives, eats, and breathes baseball. It gives him great joy. You see him gripping a ball during most of his waking hours (and maybe sometimes while he sleeps). A friend who played college ball notices that your child has a natural gift. Your son comes home from practice and wants to throw ten more pitches into the rebound net in the backyard before watching his favorite pro team on television. The game itself gives your child delight, and the person you see him becoming gives you delight.

Or maybe you begin to notice that your daughter comes alive when she has the opportunity to play volleyball. She loves spending time with the girls on her team and stays late to help another girl learn how to serve overhand. She is selected from among the best players to be on a regional team. When your family goes to the beach for vacation, she sets up a makeshift volleyball court so that your whole family can play together. You find her reading up on the history of the sport during her free time. The game gives your child delight, and the person you see her becoming gives you delight.

We simply want you to hear that—because every child is different—there aren't any formulas. Every parent needs to discern the appropriate amount of involvement that will nurture a child's development and prevent burnout or injury.

In other words, we encourage you not to *owe* your child, but to *know* your child.

A LOVING NO

When I (Dave) got home from work one day, my son Ryan came to talk with me. He was just starting seventh grade and already more than six feet tall.

"Dad," he said, "I'm going to lose nineteen pounds."

"Why would you do that?" I asked, curious.

"I want to go out for football, and I need to lose nineteen pounds to qualify for my age group."

I asked Ryan more about why he wanted to go out for football. He said a lot of his friends were, and other parents were telling him how awesome he would be. People thought he could be a wide receiver. My wife, Deb, and I know a little bit about physical development, and we decided that playing football (and losing nineteen pounds) was not a wise choice for a kid his size who was still growing. In the end, we said no.

Part of our job as parents is to see the big picture that children don't see.

HELPING A CHILD DECIDE

Sam is nine years old. His buddies in the neighborhood want him to sign up to join their town's recreation league soccer team. It's not highly competitive, and a friend's dad will be the coach. Sam's parents encourage him, and he joins the team.

Over the course of the season, Sam's experience isn't spectacular. He doesn't see a lot of playing time. When he's in the game, he often makes errors. The night after the team's final game of the season, as the family eats dinner together, Sam tells his folks, "I'm not sure if I want to play soccer next season."

And there it is.

That's the moment when the job of parenting doesn't have anything to do with what you owe your child. The job in that moment is to *know* your child.

We don't know Sam, but let's consider the possibilities.

It could be that Sam is not the least bit athletically inclined. Maybe he doesn't enjoy playing team sports or watching team sports. Maybe he's much happier baking chocolate chip cookies, playing Connect Four with a friend, or building a fort with blankets and chairs. It may be that Sam's parents decide he would be much better served if his other interests were nurtured instead of playing soccer.

It could also be that Sam is a late bloomer. Perhaps, at nine, he has not yet developed the kind of coordination that would allow him to excel in soccer. Maybe he loves the game and has a great mind for strategy but needs a few years for his body to catch up to his heart and brain. It may be that Sam's parents encourage him to play soccer in the neighborhood, take him to watch a few high school games, skip a season of rec league, and then return to it the following season.

The best they can do is to help Sam find the path that makes the most sense for him.

KNOW YOUR CHILD

During her sophomore year of high school, my (Margot's) daughter, Zoe, was agonizing over whether to play basketball. The agony lasted all the way through tryouts.

And beyond.

Zoe, ambivalent, thought she wanted to play basketball to stay in shape between volleyball and soccer, which were her true passions.

Friends who saw her show up to conditioning and tryouts were thrilled, and insisted she play.

The coaches fell in love with her pretty quickly. (I deny that it was only because Zoe is six feet tall; it was definitely her winning personality and extraordinary effort.)

I tried to act nonchalant and disinterested on the outside. But I played high school basketball, and I would have loved for Zoe to have a similar experience.

Those four competing motivations—Zoe's, friends', coaches', and mine—made it really difficult for Zoe, a thoughtful decision maker, to decide. Typical of many children, she would have loved to please her mom. Typical of many teens, she would have loved to please her friends. Typical of many athletes, she would have loved to please her coaches. What was really tangled and harder to discern was what *Zoe* actually wanted.

And the answer is nowhere in the parent handbook.

The very best I could do was make a weird, painfully creepy effort to let Zoe decide. "What if everyone—your friends, your coaches, me—were all on an airplane that crashed into an ocean?" I asked her. "Then what would you do? What would you decide if it was just you?"

Though the odd query didn't make it much easier for Zoe to choose, it may have communicated that it really was Zoe's choice and that I would honor it.

We don't owe our children any particular experience of youth sports. What we do owe them is a space to discover who they are and who they're becoming. Sometimes that happens in the backyard, and sometimes it happens in organized sports. If every parent could see into the future, the decisions would be easy. As it is, we pay attention to our kids and help them become who they were made to be. We listen to them, reflect what we see and hear, and help them make the best decisions they can make.

We do our best to honor the unique individual God has made.

Set limits early

Families who find themselves harried and overwhelmed by their children's athletic commitments often ask themselves, "How did we get here?!" Consider and make decisions about what your family will invest beforehand—when the coach hands you the schedule—not after you're caught up in it. Establishing limits early means that your family will be able to honor other important commitments to extended family, community, and church.

1. Money

Decide in advance how much money your family will devote to sports. Some families let a child know what they plan to spend on summer activities and let the child have a voice in how it's dispersed. Other parents look at their budget and decide what they can afford to spend in a year. Others go into debt. Being proactive in deciding at the front end will serve you well.

2. Time

Decide how much time your family will devote to sports. If you have more than one child, it can get a bit complicated! Some families limit each child to one team per season. Others allow each child to choose a sport to play in the fall and the spring, and skip the winter season. You may decide to join a team that does not have games on Sunday mornings, or choose to forego those games so that your family can attend church services together.

3. Physical risk

Decide how much physical risk you are willing to expose your child to. If your child is a baseball or softball pitcher, learn about the risks of overuse injuries. If your child plays football or soccer, learn about the consequences of repeated concussions. We realize there is a risk in walking across the street, and we're not advocating being overprotective. But it is important to learn about the physical risks of a certain sport or a particular position in a sport.

4. Emotional risk

Decide what kind of adults you want to have shaping your child. If there's a coach with a reputation for being verbally abusive to his players, you can draw the line at letting your child play for that coach. A more difficult call is if one of your child's parents—not you, of course!—is unable to control himself or herself on the sidelines. Just as you have an obligation to protect your child from physical harm, you also have a responsibility to protect him or her from emotional harm. Also, make sure your child's sports experiences are congruent with his or her developmental stage.

5. Loss of age-appropriate play

Decide when is the best time for your child to begin organized youth sports. Because the type of leagues available in your area matters, and because every child and family is unique, that age will be different for different children.

6. Relational costs and benefits

Decide what relational sacrifices you and your child are willing to make in order to honor any commitment you make to a team. Inherent in organized youth sports is the possibility of developing some great friendships with players and coaches. Time away from your normal orbit, however, can jeopardize existing relationships. Are you willing to take younger siblings along to out-of-town tournaments? Are you—and your child— okay with missing a family vacation with relatives? Will you help your child carve out other time to spend with a lifelong friend who won't be playing sports?

Q&A with Dave

Question: Dave, is it ever okay not to play?

Answer: This is where we as parents can really struggle, isn't it? We naturally want to give our children the best, and we feel like we owe this to them. And while I'm a big believer in the power of sports to develop children, I'm not of the mind that we owe our children any one particular experience of sports.

I can think of a number of situations when parents don't need to feel obligated in this way.

If athletic fees are out of range for a family's budget, that's a legitimate reason not to play. I want you to hear that there's no shame in that. Parents who want their children to have a great experience of sports can help facilitate free play in a neighborhood or after church at a park. I understand this may be difficult for a child to accept, but great parents who are committed to their children's well-being don't necessarily enroll them in pay-to-play sports.

Another legitimate reason for a child not to play is if you have concerns about the way a coach will interact with your child. Some parents reason, "These are the kinds of jerks she'll have to deal with in life, so I'll be there to support her." Other parents decide, "It's not worth it. She doesn't need to play for this one." As a parent, you have the right and the ability to make either call.

I'm also aware that when a child has had to skip a season or two, or when he hasn't played for the "right" teams or coaches, the politics of certain communities might actually mean that child is excluded from the next opportunity.

Although that's a hard lump for a child and parents to swallow—and I say this with loving-kindness—it's not the worst thing in the world for your child not to play for that program. It may *feel* like it's the end of the world to your child—or even to you! But I believe that you have the skills to help your child reflect on the fact that, over time, his personhood doesn't depend on it. And I would suggest that if those in charge run their program that way, the welfare of the children is subservient to building a winning program. Are you sure you want to be involved with a program that places politics over people?

I'd also like to underscore that if a child doesn't want to play a sport—because he's not wired to enjoy it, or because she has other interests about which she's much more passionate—that's legitimate! This choice may bruise a parent's pride, but that's not a good reason to push a child. If you suspect there's something else at work—that she's just nervous because it's new, or that he's anxious about playing on a team without his best friend—go ahead and push a little. Our job is to serve our children in the best ways we can.

Of course, there are many other legitimate reasons for a child to not play a sport. If it's not the right choice for your family or for your child, you need not waste a moment of worry about saying a loving, compassionate no.

Myth Two

My Child Deserves to Play with the Most-Skilled Athletes

It's the moment a few parents relish and a lot of us dread: your child comes home with the invitation letter and registration form to sign up for a club sport.

At Susan's house, the crumpled piece of paper to register her daughter to play with Cityville Volleyball Club sat on the kitchen counter for about a week. (That it had made it out of her daughter Amber's backpack was really a win, actually.) When Susan saw it, her mind flooded with a million reasons to *not* sign her daughter up for club volleyball. Amber had played for her middle school team, but Susan had heard that there was a lot of competition to play for the high school where she'd be headed the next year. She felt as though she owed her daughter the chance to play with better players so that she'd remain competitive.

But there were obstacles . . .

The *cost*. Another mom had told Susan that fees, gear, gas, and other travel opportunities could tally upward of $2,000 to $3,000.

The *time*. Cityville Volleyball Club, the only year-round volleyball opportunity in the area, was located in an office park a thirty-minute drive away.

The *energy*. A lot of days, Susan's daughter Amber was ambivalent about getting up for Saturday morning sports. Other days she could be downright ornery. Once they signed up, Susan knew she'd be the one dragging Amber out of bed on Saturday mornings and wrestling her into the family minivan. She also knew that she'd need to persuade her children to do their weekly chores and laundry in the late-night or early-morning weekday hours, since the family traveled many weekends.

The *strain*. Susan, a single mom, had two younger kids at home. Without other players nearby with whom they could carpool, Susan's other two kids were obligated to ride in the minivan for the sixty-minute round-trip—if they killed time at a nearby mall for the two hours Amber played, bringing their commitment to three hours—or two trips of sixty minutes each. Susan knew that neither option would be pleasant.

The *missed opportunities*. Susan's youngest had already missed a friend's birthday party because of her big sister's rigorous schedule, and even Amber had missed out on enrolling in a prep class for the SATs. Though they usually couldn't predict what they'd miss in a season, the family knew they'd miss out on something.

"Is it worth it?" Susan wondered. "Is it worth all of that?"

Susan knew that Amber liked playing volleyball. Realistically, though, she could also see Amber wasn't headed for the next Olympics. She might not even play for a college team. But Susan did want her to have the opportunity to play for the high school volleyball team.

The persistent mantra that kept rattling around in Susan's head was this: *she has to play with better players if she's ever going to get better.*

The nagging voice was what eventually persuaded Susan to sign Amber up for the club.

PLAYING "UP"

It's tempting to believe that our children "deserve" everything within our grasp that we can give them. It's a very subtle distortion of what it means to love our children. With the best of intentions, we make decisions based on this twisted logic.

I (Dave) had just released the middle school basketball team when Jason's dad approached me. Jason had played on my soccer team the previous year as a seventh grader, and had been a great asset to our team. I liked Jason, and it seemed like he'd really enjoyed being on the team with his friends.

"I just want to let you know," Mr. Walker began, "that Jason won't be playing soccer for the middle school team this year."

"Hmm . . ." I sighed, curious. "And why is that?"

I suspected I already knew.

"Well, he needs to play with better players, and he needs to be with better coaches."

He didn't even flinch when he said it.

"So we're going to join one of the elite travel teams in Pennsylvania," Mr. Walker continued. "I want Jason to play at Bucknell, my alma mater, and I think a scholarship is a real good possibility."

At the end of our little breakup chat, I knew exactly what Mr. Walker wanted. I was still curious, though, what Jason wanted. I had a hunch, and my hunch told me not to get involved.

Throughout middle school and high school, Jason and his dad traveled up and down the East Coast in pursuit of the dream. Jason did play for our high school team. But because he continued with travel ball during the winter, spring, and summer, he didn't play with the high school team in the summer league or attend camp with them.

Mr. Walker had dreamed of his son playing for Bucknell, a Division I school. And guess what? Jason did suit up in the Bisons' orange and blue. But only for the two weeks of preseason. After those two weeks, he was informed that he wasn't tall enough, fast enough, or strong enough to make the team.

Jason's dream, though, had been to play at the collegiate level. He could have played for any number of schools, including the Division II and Division III schools that recruited him. But instead, his dream was dashed, and he settled for playing intramural soccer. I learned this when Jason came to visit me, after college graduation, confessing that his dream had gone up in smoke. Playing in elite youth leagues, and even being successful on these teams, hadn't equipped Jason to play Division I soccer.

It seemed like such a loss. This kid was denied the opportunity to play collegiate soccer, possibly at the Division III national level, because his dad believed he needed to play with better players. In this case, and many others, playing with the elite players and programs doesn't change a player's physical and physiological limits.

Ironically, in this case, it is what *kept* him from playing.

WHAT YOU NEED TO KNOW

Is it necessary to play with better players to get better?

It's the nagging question that haunted Susan as she considered whether her daughter Amber would play club volleyball.

While there's not a simple formulaic answer, we always want to give families permission to choose an option that makes sense for their family and their values. Yes, kids will likely get better by playing with better players. But too often we identify the experience as a guarantee for something in the future, when it's not always the cause-and-effect sequence we'd like to believe it is.

The persistent myth, as we investigated in the previous chapter, is that we "owe" it to our children to give them opportunities to get to the next level. Or that playing at the next level guarantees athletic success. But it doesn't. Too often our choices have been driven by fear—that our child will "miss out"—or by the misconception that playing on the elite team ensures a player will be recruited and possibly receive a scholarship. But as Jason learned, that's simply not the case.

We "owe" it to our children to look at the needs and desires and resources of the family and make the best choice we can. We want you to hear that a good parent can decide, "The toll of this commitment is too much for the rest of our family. We're saying no this season." We want families to be able to recognize, "My child eats, sleeps, and breathes lacrosse. I see him being his best self on the field—generous, smart, kind—and this commitment is one our family will make for this season."

We even want families to be able to say, "Because our family cares deeply about the needs of the poor, and because we want to use some of our money to help alleviate poverty, we're going to make the choice to not put this much money into a sport right now." If there's anything that defies the "pattern of this world," it's suggesting that prioritizing the needs of *other* people's children—specifically those who are under-resourced—above the wants of our own children is a legitimate choice. It is a countercultural choice that some Christian families are quietly making.

Most of all, though, we want parents to hear that a thoughtful no to climbing the youth sports ladder, for any number of reasons, is a legitimate choice for good parents who love their kids.

BUT WE *PAID* FOR HER TO PLAY!

One prevailing assumption behind the myth that a child must play with better players is that he or she will necessarily improve. While that may be the case, there are no guarantees.

As a high school athletics director in the past, I (Dave) had parents come into my office indignant that their child wasn't getting a lot of playing time on our varsity team.

"I don't get it, Dave. I've taken my daughter to the camp at Penn State, she's gone to a camp at Indiana University, we got her a private instructor, and she has played on local club teams for years. And you're telling me that she's not good enough to get significant playing time on your high school team?!"

That's what I was telling them.

Students' outside experiences *don't* guarantee them a spot on the team. Sometimes a great coach on an elite or club team will help your child to be a better player by the end of the season than she was at the beginning. But playing on an elite team doesn't guarantee that your child will be able to play at the next level or will be recruited. The rosters for travel and elite teams are kept small so that coaches don't have to deal with parents who have paid big bucks demanding that their daughters get more playing time. So just because elite team members get playing time doesn't necessarily mean they're the best in the community. But the system leads families to believe it's true.

Unfortunately, travel ball doesn't always give an athlete a sense of how to get better, nor the opportunity for skill improvement. Travel ball—where a typical schedule might be to practice once or twice a week and play two or three games on a weekend—is focused on playing games and giving players exposure, not on skill development. You get better from practicing, but travel teams are more game-heavy than practice-heavy. Skill development comes best from repetition. For instance, travel baseball games only offer repetition to the pitcher and the catcher.

This approach contributes to one of the major deficiencies in first-year athletes at my university and nearly all others across the country. Young athletes come to play, but they don't understand the role and the value of practice. They don't know the importance of weight training, nutrition, sleep, and the need to develop core strength. Playing time at the collegiate level is based on an athlete's performance in practice, not the previous game.

To put it quite bluntly, the explosion of elite travel teams has forced collegiate coaches to spend more time in skill development than they should have to. It's why one of the major challenges for collegiate freshmen athletes is how much hard work it takes to get better. During the high school years, athletic development progresses as the body naturally grows bigger, faster, and more coordinated. The amount of skill development during college will be much less, but it will take at least twice as much effort. The skills are the same in high school and college, but in college the skills have to be executed with more speed, intensity, strength, and consistency.

WHAT ARE WE LOSING?

We are not the only ones who have noticed these recent deficits. Talk to any college coach today and she will tell you that the young people who are coming into college athletics have far fewer problem-solving skills than players did a few decades ago. Their creativity is basically zilch. Athletes who have simply bumped from one organized team to the next, season by season, haven't had the opportunity to develop some of the problem-solving skills that can be acquired from free play in the neighborhood.

When I (Dave) was a boy, kids in the neighborhood would meet at the empty corner lot, or out back near the barn, to play a game of baseball. A lot of parents today who grew up in the 1970s and 1980s still remember neighborhood pickup games of Wiffle ball in the street (and clearing out for the occasional passing car). But as we mentioned earlier, many parents today report that their neighborhoods are desolate. Kids aren't playing outside. And even if a parent did send her child out into the neighborhood to round up friends to play, Nick would be at practice for travel team, Sarah would be at cello lessons, and Lucy would be at dance class.

Now, I know guys like me like to wax nostalgic about the good ol' days. But I want you to hear what kids gain when they organize their own games and agree on their own rules.

They decide together whether a fly ball clearing the first window of the barn or the second window of the barn is a homer.

They calculate how to make a game fair if there's only one kid in the neighborhood who can pitch.

They have to use a flip-flop for first base, another flip-flop for second base, a glove for third base, and a piece of cardboard for home plate.

They have to figure out how to make two baseball teams with nine players in all.

One of the ways you play with a small number of kids is by using a "ghost runner." If you as a player are still on base and it's your turn to bat, the ghost runner—that is, an invisible player—takes your place on the base and you come in to bat.

So imagine you're up to bat, with a ghost runner on second. Two outs. First pitch is way out of the box. Everyone agrees it's a ball. Second pitch: you swing and miss. Strike one. But on the third pitch, right over the plate, you nail the ball into left field and take off around the bases. You're inches away from second when you're tagged out. The big existential question—the one that has no doubt produced more than one bloody nose over the years—is this: Did the ghost runner make it home before the runner was tagged out?

Kids who figure that out? Now *they* are developing problem-solving skills! They really want the game to be fair, and they figure it out as they go. And while they know who won and lost, it really isn't a big deal. Tomorrow is another day, another game, and most likely different teams.

When neighborhood kids gathered up teams, no one sat on the bench. If you wanted to play soccer and you had twenty kids, you created a big field. If you only had four, you made a small field. You changed the size of the goals. Everybody got to play. Yet in organized sports—admittedly, my bread and butter!—kids spend a lot of time standing around the sidelines. In pickup games, they likely get to play every position—and probably some that don't even exist!

I know: I'm an old guy. And I'm not trying say, "Let's turn the clock back to the good ol' days." (I can't even guarantee that they were all that good!) What I'd like you to hear is that taking free play away from our children and putting them in organized sports is not necessarily what's best for them, if it's their only experience of sport. And while I'm not advocating that we completely revert to backyard games, there are some principles that can be incorporated in other ways.

We'll get into it a bit more in the next chapter, but the breadth of an athlete's experience is really important. I love it when athletes come to my school who have developed creativity by playing backyard ball in addition to whatever organized leagues they have joined. I also like to work with athletes who have played several sports and not just specialized in one.

The assumption that specialty leagues are the only way to improve as a player simply isn't true.

BUMPING UP AGAINST OUR NATURAL LIMITS

Parents also need to know that even the most generous investment of time and money doesn't guarantee that their child won't reach the ceiling of his physical limits, like our young friend who didn't make the team at Bucknell.

A lot of people we know have been reading Malcolm Gladwell's *Outliers: The Story of Success*. In his examination of folks who have had a lot of success, Gladwell cites the ten-thousand-hour rule, which posits that the key to success in any field—music, business, athletics—is to practice a specific task for ten thousand hours. A lot of parents who are pushing their children to excel in youth sports either must have read this or are practicing the principle intuitively!

But David Epstein, author of *The Sports Gene: Inside the Science of Extraordinary Athletic Performance* and a senior writer for *Sports Illustrated*, challenges the ten-thousand-hour assumption. No, scientists haven't yet isolated a particular "sports" gene, but research has shown that people are born with an intrinsic degree of athleticism. So although we don't want our children to be doomed to achieve no more than we did, Epstein suggests that a clue to the predictor of extraordinary athletic performance might be found in the people who gave birth to us.

Although we live in a "you can be anything you want to be" culture, any number of variables—speed, height, weight, body proportions—might actually prevent your child from becoming the next Venus Williams or Lionel Messi. (Though Messi, at five foot three, which is very short for a soccer player, is a shining exception to the rule!)

It's fair to say that, in general, no amount of elite travel ball will change our inherent physical limits. Parents serve children well by helping them identify and work toward realistic goals.

For many years, we thought perfect vision was 20/20. Then we discovered that pro baseball players have *better* than 20/20 vision. In *The Sports Gene*, Epstein cites research conducted on

What if it's clear my child won't excel at a sport?

1. **If your child who is weak at a sport makes the team . . .**
   Ask how she's feeling about it. Don't assume your child will count the experience a failure just because you do. Your child might love the experience of being on a team and might enjoy the challenge of playing against better players.

2. **If your child who is weak at a sport is cut from the team . . .**
   Help your child find other strengths. Give him opportunities to explore other interests.

3. **Stay open to possibilities.**
   If your five-year-old is that kid who picks flowers in right field, or if your middle schooler doesn't make the basketball team: don't count him out too quickly. Children mature at different rates and hit their growth spurts at different times. Continue to notice and gauge your child's interest in the activity.

the Los Angeles Dodgers by Louis Rosenbaum, former team ophthalmologist for the NFL's Arizona Cardinals:

> Over four years of testing [of] 387 major and minor league players, Rosenbaum found an average visual acuity around 20/13. Position players (players who have to hit) had better vision than pitchers and major league players had better vision than minor leaguers. . . . 58% of baseball players scored "superior" in the test of fine depth perception compared to only 18% of the control population. . . . In each eye test pro baseball players were better than non-athletes and major league players were better than minor league players.

Now as I (Dave) reflect on the years when my kids were younger, I think differently about my shouts of encouragement, "Keep your eye on the ball!" Perhaps I was asking my kids to do something they may not have been *physically* able to do: see the ball well enough to hit it. So while practice is valuable, there will always be some physical limitations in skill development.

A PLUG FOR PLAYING WITH LESS-SKILLED PLAYERS

While we're discussing the benefits—real and perceived—of playing with more-skilled players, we have to give a plug for playing with less-skilled players.

Playing with less-skilled players—in the neighborhood, on school teams, or in organized leagues outside of school—helps young people learn self-awareness. The inherent nature of athletic competition gives young people a unique opportunity to compare themselves to others. They come to understand, in a more full way, who they are in relation to those around them. They discover how they react when they win and when they lose. (Hint: You have to lose to discover how you react when you lose. It's really not the worst thing in the world.)

These players can also learn how to help others. This is one of those areas where the world's values are different from the values knit into the kingdom Jesus ushered in. While the world drives kids to be the best that they can be, always putting self at the center, playing with less-skilled players allows more-experienced athletes to share their expertise and encouragement.

Playing with less-skilled players also gives children and teens the chance to recognize and value the contributions each person on the team can make. Instead of driving to be the singular hotshot on the team, young people can learn to understand teamwork in a more meaningful way.

Though players who are surrounded by teammates who aren't as skilled may be tempted to let their big-fish-in-a-small-pond success go to their heads, the fact that they won't be winning as many games might keep them humble! But the great lesson that attentive coaches and parents can be teaching these stronger athletes is that they're really competing against themselves. These athletes can be encouraged to be the best that they can be, without comparison.

The experience of a child playing on a "losing team" gives parents an opportunity to know a side of their child they might not otherwise have the opportunity to see. Parents have a chance to observe how their child reacts to other authority figures, or to the player on the team who is the least competent, or to the kid who is a bragger. Granted, being on a losing team might not be as fantastic as we make it sound here, but honestly: it really is a unique opportunity.

STREET SOCCER

Today, the best soccer players in the world aren't the ones whose parents shelled out cash every season so they could work their way up to a regional all-star game. The best male soccer players in the world today are the ones who grew up playing soccer on the street!

These are the little guys who started kicking around a rotten grapefruit or a wadded-up ball of grocery bags in the dusty alley behind their homes. They started scrapping, as five-year-olds, with boys who were nine, and twelve, and even eighteen! When these guys started out, they weren't picked first on teams, but they learned from hard knocks. Many of these players were scouted out in the cities of South America or Africa and then invited to play in European club academies, where they study and are groomed into professional players. It's interesting that while the U.S. men's soccer team has improved its competitiveness in the World Cup competition, the efforts in the United States to establish elite clubs and enroll young players in Olympic development programs and academies have not resulted in a championship—or even a top-four finish—in the last four men's World Cup competitions.

When I (Margot) got the chance to sit in on an elite basketball camp, which had gathered up some of the best high school players in the United States, it was a decidedly pale group. I couldn't help but wonder why this group of the "best" high school players in the country looked so demographically different from the NBA, which is rich with people of color. Though some players in the NBA do have stories of going to prestigious summer camps during high school, a lot more players in the NBA don't. Like their international counterparts, a lot of these guys improved by playing against older, taller, faster guys in their neighborhoods.

In response to the increased number of foreign-born players in the NBA, Kobe Bryant has remarked that he believes European basketball players are more skilled than American players are. During a recent interview, Bryant—who was raised in Europe, where his father played professional basketball—blamed the decline in skilled players in the United States on its popular Amateur Athletic Union programs. He believes that the AAU teams don't teach kids how to play the game. While these players come out of AAU performing some fancy tricks, Bryant believes they often fail to display mastery of fundamentals. His solution? Teach players the fundamental skills of the game at an early age and spend less time playing games and tournaments. Bryant doesn't expect things to change very quickly, though, given the amount of money that is involved in AAU.

Curious about the difference between the elite high school players and the ones playing in the NBA, we poked around a bit. We discovered that the players on the field of the host university in Chicago had all been selected from elite regional teams across the United States. And the players in the elite regional teams had been selected by coaches of elite local teams. So in order to have made it to the high school "big leagues," players had to have paid to play locally, paid to play regionally, and then paid to fly to the Windy City, ideally with a parent, during one week in the summer. Suddenly, the pale-complexioned teams made more sense.

If you want your child to play with "better" players to improve his or her skills, such players might be found in local elite leagues. But they also might be hidden in neighborhoods or playgrounds near you.

STORY OF A SUCCESSFUL PLAYER WHO DIDN'T CLIMB THE LADDER

We mentioned that Todd Phillips was the first All-American basketball player at Eastern Mennonite University where I (Dave) work. This young man was unbelievably talented. It was a joy to watch Todd in action on the court.

One of the most important parts of Todd's game was his creativity. The way he was able to see what was happening on the court, with and without the ball, and get in position to get his shot off, was remarkable.

Todd was also a gifted ball handler. On one hand, ballhandling is a physical skill. But Todd had a unique instinct to recognize where the ball needed to be in order to be most effective for the team, and then to get the ball there. He had the ability to make moves around defenders and even a superhero-esque ability to hang in the air during a shot.

Todd never played AAU basketball in high school, the way a lot of folks thought he should have—or simply assumed that he had! Todd's game was developed at his backyard hoop and in pickup games. In organized sports, players are, understandably, expected to run their coach's plays. But not being formed in that way allowed Todd to develop his unique creativity and dynamic problem-solving skills. And we're convinced that the neural connections between his eyes, brain, and muscles operated at higher levels and with greater efficiency than ours. His ability to hit off-balance shots may have been based on a higher-level functioning of his motor neurons, which told his arm muscles how hard to push the basketball given his position on the court and in relation to the basket and the defender.

We believe that Todd's unique skills developed because he *hadn't* been indoctrinated by organized sports!

ONE LEGIT REASON TO PLAY WITH MORE-SKILLED PLAYERS

Just as we gave a pitch for playing with less-skilled players, we also recognize a surprising benefit—beyond the development of physical skills—of playing against *more*-skilled players.

As a high school athletics director, I (Dave) had the unique opportunity to watch my children play high school sports—at

least the home games, as my wife, Deb, was the traveling parent. My daughter, Lisa, played field hockey and basketball for
four years, and softball for one. During the fall of Lisa's senior
year, she had a wonderful experience as the captain of the field
hockey team. They had a very successful season, and they made
it to the state championship game.

As field hockey ended, she picked up a basketball to finish
her final season of high school athletics. Lisa had started for
the junior varsity team as a sophomore and continued to be a
strong player during her junior year on the varsity team. At the
end of the season, Lisa had been selected as one of the team
captains for the following year. The successful trajectory of her
senior year was right on course.

During preseason, Lisa rarely saw much playing time among
the starting five players. She assumed this was because she
wasn't able to participate in the open gyms during the fall when
she was playing field hockey. It normally took her a few weeks
to get into "basketball shape." Some of the players had been improving their skills and becoming better players. And when the
season began, the senior captain wasn't in the starting lineup.
For the rest of the season, she never started and she didn't see
much playing time. One of the other captains was in a similar
situation.

When Lisa had started playing ball as a sophomore, there
hadn't been as many talented players on the court. But the competition had increased. Suddenly younger players were starting
ahead of Lisa.

It certainly wasn't what Lisa had planned for her senior year.
She was frustrated. She shed a lot of tears. She worked hard in
practice. She talked with the coach. (I have a lot of respect for
this coach, whose tough decision not to put the senior captain
in the starting lineup was likely only tougher because I, Lisa's

dad, was his boss!) How can you be a leader when you're not the best player? And how can you be a leader when you're not even on the floor? These leadership questions were being asked by both the team and the two captains. It was a painful but valuable experience for everyone.

Over the course of the season, I noticed how Lisa navigated these challenges. I saw her make the player ahead of her better by hustling on the court and playing as hard as she could in practice. I watched her experience that aha moment when she could authentically cheer for the girl who was playing ahead of her, knowing that she had helped her get better. The team learned how to follow someone who wasn't in the middle of them. Lisa discovered that she'd helped and served her team with a different style of leadership. And I don't think it was until the final celebration banquet with the team that Lisa, and others, understood the important lessons she and the team had experienced.

Today, as she transitions from a nurse manager position in Lancaster, Pennsylvania, to teaching in a university nursing department, Lisa will tell you that that season was one of the experiences that molded her into the leader she is today.

So, in some cases, it really is important to play with more-skilled players. Maybe just not in the way that the myth teaches us to expect.

WHEN TO PLAY WITH THE BEST

Overall, however, the hype about opportunities missed by not aggressively pushing kids up the pyramid when they're young just isn't true. In countless conversations with coaches at all levels, we have found that most coaches agree that seventh grade is a good time to start participating in travel teams. Tenth or eleventh grade is when kids can begin to specialize.

The strongest support for these ideas comes from collegiate coaches. Parents who are eager for their kids to achieve athletically might be glad to hear that it's not a question of *if* the elite travel team but *when*.

Kathy and Mike are a couple in my (Margot's) church. Kathy played basketball for West Virginia University and Mike played for Pacific Lutheran University. Mike has a master's degree in sports science and has coached at the high school and college level over the last twenty-five years. So sports really are their thing.

When their son, Jay, was eight, he joined a basketball team through a local church. While the action was happening at one end of the court, Jay would practice Power Ranger kicks alone at the other end. (Every coach-dad's dream.) In middle school, Jay played some baseball and ran track to be with his friends.

Jay continued playing basketball, along with a few other sports, with fewer and fewer power kicks on the court. In eighth grade, Jay told his parents that he wanted to play only basketball. Although they understood the benefits of being a multisport athlete, they allowed Jay to make that decision. By the time Jay began high school, he was six feet four inches tall. As you might imagine, AAU coaches began calling Mike and Kathy to invite Jay to play for their teams. Knowing their boy, they declined.

"That's not who he was," Mike explains.

Jay was loving basketball by this point, Mike clarifies, but even in early high school, Jay wouldn't have thrived with the rigorous schedule required by more competitive leagues. "He liked his free time," Mike says. "He liked playing with friends."

The big win for Jay is that his parents knew who he was and were able to separate that out from who they were. (They're both "competitive" athletes. Truly, they're fierce.) Evidence of their good choices is that both Jay and his sister, Katrina—at eighteen and nineteen—are still enjoying their sports.

Today, at six feet ten inches tall, Jay is a high school senior. And a great baller. He's played AAU and also plays for his high school team, coached by his dad. As you might imagine, the family is now getting a few phone calls from interested colleges. Though Jay hasn't decided where he'll play yet, his parents are guiding him as he chooses a school.

For starters, they want it to be a school he'd choose to attend even if he wasn't playing ball. They're also putting a priority on Jay finding a school where he can develop a good relationship with a coach. Mike knew a number of guys who played Division I ball and, because of some rough coaches, had a really bad experience.

Coach Mike's hopes for his son?

"At the end of four years, I'd like for him to have had an experience that helped him become a better man. To have been part of something bigger than himself. I hope he enjoys it and has great memories."

Jay's experience speaks to the question, is it important for every child to play with better players to improve? Now that Jay is moving toward college ball, it *is* time for him to be playing with the best. But when he was eight, nine, and ten, he was playing for fun and also having fun with his friends. He continued to grow as a player because he is gifted, he has worked hard, and he has the good basketball fortune of being almost seven feet tall.

As you decide whether your child needs to play against better players to improve his game, to train with better athletes who will push her to excel, know your child and let him or her be your guide.

WE DON'T ALWAYS KNOW WHO IS THE MOST-SKILLED

We also want parents to hear that we don't always know who the most-skilled players are.

My (Dave's) son Ryan, who is now six foot nine, was about six feet tall in the fifth grade. So you can imagine that, like Jay, he was also pretty popular among coaches seeking players. It's not that he was good, but he was tall. And because he was tall, he didn't have to work at developing the skills to be successful. He didn't have to work at positioning for rebounds: he just got them. He didn't have to work at the concepts of the game because he was just . . . well . . . big. He wasn't forced to get better. He was good enough for the travel team.

He played throughout high school and college. In high school his team went to the final four of the state tournament, losing to a team with a Division I recruit who was seven foot one. He played two years at a junior college before ending up at Eastern Mennonite University. I heard a few folks comment that he never developed into the kind of player they'd expected him to become. Notice that I said who *they* expected him to become. Too often we put expectations on kids based on their early years. What matters is that Ryan was satisfied with his basketball experiences in both high school and college, despite others' expectations.

We've seen similar situations in which adults had excessively high expectations for other athletes. These parents decide—when the child is seven or eight or nine—that he's good. Maybe a coach tells the parents the child is good, and they get stars in their eyes. (Maybe dollar signs too.) Then in high school the parents are yelling at the coaches for not playing the kid or for not selecting him to play varsity.

The reality, though, is that development happens at a variety of rates. A child who is used to shining on the field or the court is passed by a late bloomer. So we're making decisions about our children's abilities based on a wrong perception.

While coaching junior high basketball, I (Dave) had a young man on my team who, simply put, *dominated* the season. He could do everything. He'd get the rebound and dribble the length of the court and score. He was Mr. Everything in basketball. And naturally, the expectations were high.

But some funny things happened on the way to high school. The game got more complicated. Players began to develop and catch up with him. The opponents were better. The high school game was quite different. And he struggled. It took him an extra long time to learn the plays, understand the defensive rotations, and read what the defense gave him. And his father wore out the coaching staff with his incessant conversations about his son's performance and his playing time. His son was great as junior high player but average, at best, as a high school player.

While we understand that Mr. Everything's dad might naturally have expected him to continue to excel in basketball—and many parents operate under the same assumption—early success in sports isn't necessarily a predictor of success at older ages. Many parents assume that the star who sparkles at age nine or ten will be the one who shines at eighteen. But that just isn't true. We're not saying that your nine-year-old isn't a good player. He or she very well may be a strong player in relation to his or her teammates and opponents, but that doesn't automatically translate into later success.

And the converse is true as well: we may assume a child doesn't have an aptitude for a particular sport at seven or eight or nine years old. But that child might very well develop and excel a few years later.

IF YOU SAY NO

If you weigh your values and commitments and decide to say no to that team that will get your child to the next level, we're not saying that it'll be easy.

Jonathan was ten when his friends begged him to join the travel team they'd be playing on over the summer. In direct proportion to their begging, Jonathan began begging his dad, Frank, to allow him to play.

After weighing a lot of factors—time, money, other commitments, the family's values and priorities—Frank and his wife said no to travel ball. They explained to Jonathan that even beyond the financial cost, they weren't willing to miss some of the events they'd have to miss if he played: church activities, neighborhood potlucks, and several family get-togethers.

Understandably, Jonathan was disappointed. He even cried for a bit. But after he was done, his dad tells us that they never heard another word about it.

Frank and his family ended up getting together with several other families they knew from church and school and creating a team that played against that traveling team! They became the bosses of their team's schedule, allowing them to participate in the other parts of life that they valued, and everybody had fun.

Sure, fun is fun. But you might still be harboring the lingering question, "What if the nasty rumor I've heard from other parents is actually true: that if my son doesn't play in the elite program he won't play for his high school?" Perhaps you've heard that from other anxious parents on the bench. Maybe you'll hear it from club coaches. Maybe your daughter heard it from her best friend's older sister.

Though we don't think this is a prevalent reality, let's imagine for a moment that it is. (If it is, it's based on politics, not skill.) Let's say that, in your community, if your child doesn't start working his way up the pyramid at age six or seven, he won't play for his high school team.

So what?

We know it doesn't sound very sophisticated, but it's important for you to hear! If the very worst outcome of your child not playing increasingly competitive sports is that he can't represent his high school on the playing field, that is not world ending. It may be disappointing, to your child and to you, but it's not worth compromising the values you hold dear to make it happen.

That may not be what you or your child wants to hear. And although it may *feel* like the end of the world to your child, it's your job to live as if it's not the end of the world.

It's really not.

KATRINA THE FISH

If you choose not to move your child up to the next level of competition, you can expect other parents to question your decision. (Either to your face or behind your back.)

Jay's older sister, Katrina, a college freshman, has been swimming since . . . before she could swim. During her earliest summers, Katrina spent hours on end stretched out splashing in a baby pool on the front porch of the family's home. Her mother, Kathy, reports, "She was such a fish." She really was. She loved the water. She loved swimming. She had the long, lean frame of a swimmer. Anyone who knew Katrina could see that she was made to swim. She worked hard and was consistently dropping time. (Nonswimmers: "dropping time" is not like dropping a bag of groceries. It's actually a good thing.)

And though Katrina was swimming five days a week, she wasn't being pushed the way some other swimmers were being pushed by their families. And in the bleachers, Kathy felt the disdain of more aggressive parents.

She explains, "When I was around these parents, I felt like I was lower class. They treated me like I had no aspirations for my child. Like I wasn't committed and that we didn't have high enough goals for our daughter." Unmoved, Kathy just found her niche, and her spot in the bleachers, with parents who shared her values.

Katrina swam throughout her years in high school, and when it was time for her to look at colleges, her times were good enough to swim for a number of college teams. But Katrina realized that if she chose to swim in college, it would consume her college experience. (A visit with one college coach—eager to circumvent regulations limiting swimmers to twenty hours of practice a week—confirmed this.) Katrina decided, instead, to choose a school with a club team. Today, at nineteen, the woman who could have earned a college scholarship now pays dues to practice four days a week and compete in meets against other schools.

Katrina, the fish, still enjoys swimming. Her continued enjoyment is a testament, we believe, to both wise Katrina *and* her parents.

Just as Jay and Katrina's parents helped each to navigate the right path for them, and recognized different paths, you serve your child best by helping him or her to find the competitive (or not) option that makes the most sense for *who your child is*. As you employ your Christian values in making those thoughtful decisions, you also challenge the myth that the child of a parent reading this book—someone with the time and resources to read a book!—is "deserving" of something that is, for any child, a real privilege.

The one question you can't *not* ask

We know that there are a lot of opportunities available to your child. We also know that your child might be very, very persuasive when he or she begs. As your family considers which opportunities to pursue and decline—saying yes and saying no—the most important question you can ask is, "Why—what is the purpose of this activity?"

Let your child have a voice. Ask, "Why do you want to do this?" Then listen. She might say she wants to have fun. He might say he loves the sport. She might say she doesn't want to be the only friend not playing. He might not be able to come up with a reason at all. Read between the lines as you listen to your child. Three days or eight weeks after you've made your decision, knowing the reasons you've said yes or no is a gift to you and to your child.

In addition to children being able to answer why, parents need to be able to do the same.

Honest answers to "Why?" that might lead to a yes:

- I value my child having opportunities for exercise.

- I value my child participating in an activity with a friend.

- I know my child loves sports and thrives as an athlete.

- I want my child to have fun playing.

- I want my child to learn more about herself.

- I want my child to learn some skills.

- I want my child to build relationships with other children.

- I want my child to have every opportunity available to improve.

Honest answers to "Why?" that might lead to a no:

- This league requires more practice and game time than our family schedule will comfortably allow.

- My child is already playing another sport during this same season.

- My child is making a transition at the same time—to a new school, to a harder level of math—and will need extra time after school and in the evenings to manage new responsibilities.

- My child should play so that he or she is not the odd one out.

- My child takes music lessons that she enjoys, and I want to make sure she learns how to manage a schedule so that she doesn't get overwhelmed.

- I don't like what I've heard about the intensity level of this particular league.

- We'd have to travel too far for practices and games, and we want to use our resources differently.

Tip: Know why you've said yes or no.

Q&A with Dave

Question: So are you saying that in your ideal world, no one cares about winning and everyone gets a trophy?

Answer: No. That's not the critique I'm making. I believe in equipping kids with skills, in working hard to improve, and in pursuing excellence. You don't become successful in business if you don't work hard, become the best businessperson you can be, and develop the best product you can. In the same way, it's good for kids to learn to play hard, practice skills, and contribute to their team.

But these things have to be done at the right time and in ways that are congruent with the developmental stages of kids. Healthy competition isn't the problem. Misguided and over-zealous adults who don't really have the best interest of children in mind are the problem. When children are being diminished, when their relationships with their parents are beginning to suffer, when families are being overwhelmed: these are the things I'm calling into question.

As for the issue of trophies, I think it's best to refrain from giving any trophies until high school, when team trophies are presented to the school for league, district, or state championships determined through a playoff process. Trophies can easily become one of the extrinsic rewards that inhibit the development of the intrinsic value of "love of the game," especially when given to all players and at an early age. This diminishes the value of playing the game and means little.

Presenting individual trophies also makes public the comparison of children, which most of them are not developmentally ready to handle. (And I've experienced enough sports camps, games, and tournaments to know that most *parents* aren't ready to deal with the public comparison of children either—especially theirs!) Coaches who try to select the "best" player in a number of categories will never win with the players or the parents.

Myth Three

My Child Should Specialize in One Sport

When Sandra's son Kyle was six, she saw the way he lit up when he played baseball. When he wasn't playing catch with a friend, he was throwing a ball against a toss back in the backyard. He loved the sport so much that he rooted for the Chicago Cubs. He loved it *that* much.

Wanting him to have every opportunity, Sandra let him play baseball every season it was offered by various leagues in town, including travel ball. Throughout elementary school, they gave it all they had—time, money, passion. Kyle eventually played for his middle school team.

When he tried out for his high school team, which had a great reputation as a winner on the diamond, he didn't make the team. Sandra, surprised and disappointed, had never considered that possibility. Baseball was a big deal in the suburb where they lived, and many other boys had pushed as hard as Kyle had.

Kyle was less disappointed about the loss than Sandra was. He was happy to bow out and didn't want to continue playing club ball.

This story made us really curious about what Kyle's experience of the sport had been. So we asked Sandra if Kyle had really loved baseball and whether he missed it.

"He's told me several times that he doesn't miss it," she offered. "At all. I'd guess that it is more about the time and stress of several practices and games each week, plus the fact that he wasn't good enough to get a lot of playing time on the high-competition teams."

Then, reflecting on Kyle's experience, she added, "Also, I was not fond of his coach, who never uttered an encouraging word to anyone, as far as I heard."

The pieces began to fall into place: Excessive time commitment. Stress. Rejection. Little playing time. Bad coach.

This perfect storm for burnout and dropout, when children specialize in a sport too early, is one too many families are experiencing. The pressure to specialize in one sport is one of the most powerful forces driving families today, and it's a myth we would love to dispel.

GOOD INTENTIONS, CAUTIONARY OUTCOMES

We are concerned for young people as we see more and more children specializing early in one sport. Some are actually playing for four teams, in one season, in the same sport! Not only are these players sometimes limited to one sport; sometimes very young players are even limited to one position. If a coach decides a child is a catcher, or a first baseman, or a shortstop, that child is typically not afforded the chance to try out other positions. The goal of youth sports should be to learn the basic skills of the game, not to learn a particular position.

Specialization is beginning at younger and younger ages. That select T-ball teams of six-year-olds are traveling out of state to a tournament is a red flag! This early specialization is a function of the dream of the elusive college scholarship, which we'll discuss more later in the book. Though it might not even be conscious, parents seem to believe that throwing all their eggs in one basket—developing a child's skills in one sport, at the expense of others—will benefit their child.

We believe that most parents do want what's best for their children. Maybe a child is begging to play one more season, and a parent feels she has to cut other sports out for the good of the family. Maybe a parent knows his child so well that he realizes if his child wasn't playing year-round soccer, his eyes would be riveted on the television set with an Xbox controller glued to his hands. Maybe the child wants to do travel league with her friends. We are not questioning a parent's intentions.

Yet we do recognize the results of this early specialization: athletes who are burned out by age nineteen or twenty, players who grow to loathe their sport, college students who are awakening to what they've lost because of a rigorous schedule throughout childhood. Because of what I (Dave) see when working with college athletes, we want parents to become aware of the realities of early specialization.

THE LITTLE PICTURE AND THE BIG PICTURE

We all know that if you want to become a good piano player, you practice playing the piano. If you want to become a good basketball player, you practice playing basketball. We're not arguing with that.

The problem is that many of us can get tunnel vision and fail to see the bigger picture. The family down the street is raving about a great coach their daughter had. Or a coach calls to invite your son to play for his team. And in the moment, signing up for the team seems like a great idea.

But in the moment, we're not lifting our eyes to notice the reasons specializing might not be the right choice, in the long run, for our children—either because it could be detrimental or because another choice could benefit them *more*.

As we have traveled around, talking to parents and coaches, we've tried to discover the root of the pressure to play one sport year-round.

The kids tell us the coaches want it.

The coaches tell us the parents want it.

The parents tell us the kids want it.

We get it. It's easy to believe that the idea is coming from someone else. But it also seems that no one wants to take responsibility for their actions.

If you're a kid, and you realize that a certain coach or team wants you to play for them, you want to play for that coach or team since they are known as the best in your area.

If you run a dance studio and you send your protégé off to play volleyball, she might not come back to the dance studio when her season ends.

If you're a parent, and your child is begging you and promising that she'll never, ever, *ever* complain about going to practice, you want to give her the chance to play.

And in that moment—the night the coach calls, or your child begs, or you just want to get your kid off the couch—you reason that specializing in one sport year-round won't do your child any harm. Maybe, you think, it will even be good for him.

But take a moment to step back and look at the big picture.

When a child plays soccer, soccer, soccer, soccer—four seasons in a row, year after year—there's a good possibility he'll burn out. It's why neither of us lets our kids eat a whole tub of ice cream!

As you survey the big picture, which is what we're seeing, you might notice one of two things. First, specializing in year-round sports might actually harm your child (like too much of anything can).

Second, there might be something that's even better for her.

SOMEONE ELSE BENEFITS

The elite travel leagues that are the engine behind single-sport specialization aren't nonprofits. These leagues make money. And they depend on recruiting kids—who are typically honored to be recruited—to make money.

We're not saying that the majority of organizations have ill intentions. And if you're raising the next Lionel Messi, Gabby Douglas, or Michael Jordan, we're not suggesting that your child isn't skilled. He or she may very well be. But the reality is that in the world of youth sports, someone is making money. It might not be your child's coach, but it may be a tournament organizer you'll never know. Someone is benefiting from your child registering for his or her program. League organizers benefit. Tournament organizers benefit. Private coaches benefit. Personal trainers who offer conditioning, flexibility, and strength training benefit. The manager of the facility where the event is held benefits. The owner of the hotel where your family is required to stay benefits. We just want to help you be sure that your child is also benefiting.

We also want to clarify that elite travel teams are offering "exposure" rather than practice and skill development. You'll notice this in the high costs of attending tournaments or show-cases promising the presence of college coaches.

It's flattering for a young athlete—and her parents!—when coaches want her on their team. Whether the coach's son is begging your son at school or whether the coach calls you at home, it feels good to be wanted.

When my (Margot's) son Rollie was about eight years old, a recruiter left a message on our family's answering machine stating that she'd gotten Rollie's name for a children's model talent search. We had no idea where this recruiter had gotten his name and just laughed it off. A few months later, the modeling agency called back. And about six months later, they called back again.

Although nothing about Rollie modeling the latest fashions made any sense, and although I clearly understood that the calls could only be some wily moneymaking scheme, I still felt very flattered by the agency's persistence. And I almost began to believe that maybe Rollie did have modeling talent that I'd just never noticed.

No, we're not saying that all leagues are a scam, or that parents are falling for a hoax. But we *are* saying that being pursued by coaches can be very flattering. And enticing.

KID-DRIVEN OR BUSINESS-DRIVEN?

Melissa Walsh, the mom and sometimes coach of four hockey players and the author of *The Rookie Hockey Mom*, has seen the way kids are pushed to specialize in the sport her family loves. When Walsh and other coaches received their USA Hockey coaching certification, they were trained that kids should be well rounded athletically, playing winter sports, like hockey, in the winter, and spring and summer sports, like baseball or lacrosse, after the hockey season ends. And yet Walsh sees something different in play. She explains, "The youth hockey business model pushes a year-round approach that leads to burn out for the kids and their parents."

Of course, it's not just hockey. Every sport has its own version of elite play at local, regional, and national levels, which operate as for-profit businesses. Those businesses depend on children specializing in one sport. As parents, we know what's best for kids. Yet children and families are being bullied by those who want to make a buck.

The ones who are paying, though, are our children.

OVERUSE INJURIES

In 1974, orthopedic surgeon Frank Jobe, a physician for the Los Angeles Dodgers, performed a surgery known as ulnar collateral ligament reconstruction on left-handed pitcher Tommy John. In the surgery that has come to be known as Tommy John surgery, the surgeon opens up the arm around the elbow and drills tunnels into the humerus and ulna. A tendon, harvested from elsewhere in the patient's body, is then woven through the tunnels.

Following his surgery, John missed the entire 1975 season. After returning in 1976, he went on to win 164 more games before retiring in 1989 at the age of forty-six.

Dr. Jobe had speculated that the chances of success for Tommy John were one in a hundred. Today the success rate for Tommy John surgery has risen to closer to 90 percent.

Furthermore, respected orthopedic surgeon James Andrews reports that high school kids getting the surgery outnumber the professionals. Andrews challenges some of the assumptions of parents committed to early specialization for their child athletes in his recent book, *Any Given Monday*. This is a must-read for every parent and coach involved in youth sports. Andrews reports, "There was a tenfold increase in Tommy John at the high school/youth level in my practice since 2000. I'm doing way more of these procedures than I want to." Andrews calls the number of surgeries being performed on youth in America an epidemic. And unfortunately, these kids don't weather the surgery like the pros do. About 25–30 percent of them are no longer playing baseball two years after their surgery.

Did you hear that? Why would a talented surgeon be doing more operations than he wants to? He's doing them because more and more young athletes are suffering from overuse injuries. Not only are some of the most talented players not making it to the pros; they're not making it onto college teams because they've blown out their arms or wrists or shoulders by the time they're sixteen.

This high rate of injury is directly related to specialization. Andrews explains, "Children are pigeonholed into one sport fairly early on, which means they have very little variation in terms of muscles and joints employed and skills practiced, which can lead to fatigue and a much higher rate of injury."

Andrews understands the physiology of children's bodies. And he challenges popular myths in sports, explaining, "A common philosophy in training for sports is that 'more is better': in other words, if pitching a ball twenty times is good, pitching it forty times is twice as good. That's simply not true. 'No pain, no gain' should have no place in youth sports. Young athletes should not participate with pain." Pain exists for a reason: to warn our bodies when something is wrong. And it is likely that the wrong is physiological.

Andrews notes, "When an imbalance between strength and flexibility occurs, the injury pattern for overuse injuries increases rapidly. Young athletes who are still developing and growing often have bone malalignment, which simply means that the bones are growing at a rate that temporarily puts them out of the normal position in relation to their joints. This condition makes young athletes even more prone to overuse injuries."

We recently read a story about a baseball manager who wanted to find Frank Jobe and punch him in the nose. While we appreciate his passion, Dr. Jobe really isn't the problem. Kids aren't the problem. Adults—coaches and parents—are the problem.

While it may be tempting to simply reason that "accidents happen," a large number of overuse injuries can be correlated to the demands of organized sports, especially as a result of early specialization. Lindsey Barton Straus, who writes about youth sports safety, observes, "Left to themselves, children engaged in spontaneous and unstructured sport and recreational activity are generally free of overuse injury." The *Clinical Journal of Sport Medicine* reports that things change when adults step in.

Evidence confirms that the risk is highest for athletes participating in a sport year-round. A recent study shows that high school athletes who participate in a sport year-round have a 42 percent higher rate of injury than those who participate in three or fewer seasons per year.

When Atlanta Braves pitcher John Smoltz was welcomed into the Baseball Hall of Fame in 2015—the first Major League Baseball pitcher having had Tommy John surgery to be inducted—he paused at the end of his acceptance speech to caution families about the procedure. "I want to encourage the families and parents that are out there that this is not normal to have a surgery at fourteen and fifteen years old. [I want to encourage you] that you have time, that baseball is not a year-round sport. That you have an opportunity to be athletic and play other sports." And with a tender concern for children, he pleaded, "They're competing and maxing out too hard, too early, and that's why we're having these problems. Please, take care of those great future arms."

We understand that parents and coaches are not trying to harm children. The way to protect them is to do exactly what you're doing now: educating yourself about the realities of youth sports.

KIDS DESERVE MORE

Joe is a pitcher. His arm started bothering him when he was about nine. He kept playing, and by the time he is twelve, it is giving him more trouble.

In one game, at the bottom of the fifth inning, Joe reports, "Coach, my arm's really hurting."

Any parent knows that for him to have said something to the coach means it is pretty bad.

Both Joe and the coach know that whoever might replace Joe isn't as reliable in terms of striking out batters.

"We're just about there," the coach encourages Joe. "Can you give us one more inning? Just one more, come on, go ahead. Get out there and give me one more. You can rest all next week." Who's going to say no?

Joe goes back out to the mound for the sixth. But by the time he's sixteen, there are no more pitches left in him. His elbow—which was designed to last a lifetime—is shot.

There have always been arguments in youth baseball about throwing a curveball too early. Many believed that throwing curveballs would damage the arm. Author and surgeon James Andrews, though, insists that the most damage is done to the arm by throwing too many pitches. While some youth baseball leagues are instituting pitch counts and required rest periods, most of these apply only to games and don't include practices. And many leagues have no limits. As with Joe, both parents and coaches encourage "just a few more." What child, who naturally wants to please both parents and coaches, will have the courage to say no?

Sadly, we are blindly behaving as if these nine- and ten-year-olds have the bodies of twenty-five-year-olds. The growth spurts that children go through make them particularly vulnerable to injury. When I (Dave) come across a college athlete whose body simply can't take the physical demands of the collegiate game, I wonder how much is a result of joint, ligament, and muscle damage caused by overuse at critical developmental times.

The baseball coach at my university has pitch count limits for every pitcher, based on when the pitcher last threw and how he pitched. If only adults would demonstrate the same level of care for younger children, there would probably be a lot more good pitchers available for our baseball team! But at the tail end of childhood, when young bodies still need to be protected, many high school athletic regulatory associations are lifting restrictions on off-season practice. Because these protective boundaries have become too difficult to police, many states have thrown up their hands and said anything goes. These decisions have elicited conflict between coaches in the same school and have stimulated pressure by high school coaches for players to specialize in one sport year-round.

The belief that jumping into youth sports with both feet is the best choice, or only choice, for your child: well, it simply isn't true. In fact, most college coaches will tell you that waiting to specialize until a young athlete is a sophomore or junior in high school is sufficient to produce a strong college athlete.

When we allow our children to engage in ways and at rates that put their bodies at increased risk, we also jeopardize their enjoyment of and continuation in a sport they once loved and might continue to enjoy under the right circumstances.

SOMETHING BETTER

What if there was an alternative to year-round specialization for your child that would not only reduce her chance of injury but also actually provide benefits she wouldn't get otherwise?

That would be a win, right?

There is something like that: being a multisport athlete. Now before you accuse us of creating an even more hectic schedule for your family by advocating for playing more than one sport, please hear us out.

Variety and creativity

More and more college coaches are recognizing that athletes who played multiple sports throughout high school arrive on campus better prepared to compete than those who specialized early. Coaches often recognize in these players a creativity that's lacking in athletes who have simply been trained to run coaches' plays or perform as coaches have instructed. And, as you might expect, young athletes who played multiple sports are arriving in better shape because they haven't suffered the same kinds of overuse injuries coaches see in players who specialized early.

When Clark Humphreys, associate head coach of the track program at Vanderbilt University, recruits students out of high school, he's wary of those who have done nothing but track since middle school. He says, "I want them to be wrestlers and soccer players and softball players. I want them to have done as many sports as they could. I don't want them to come to me with four or five years of strictly track training."

Of those athletes Coach Humphreys has accepted into his program who have not done other sports, he reflects, "Some have worked out and some haven't. In terms of excelling through college and continuing on, though, it's better to have played a variety of sports."

Humphreys's observation holds up. Among the players on the U.S. women's soccer team that recently won the women's World Cup, almost half were dual-sport athletes in high school.

Humphreys encourages parents, "Open up the opportunities, give them windows to everything. Let them go play the piano. Play football. Do 4-H. Let the options be plentiful. Get them there and then see which ones they gravitate toward." It's a philosophy he and his wife have implemented with their own children. He explains, "My wife and I continually check in with the kids and ask them, 'Is it fun?' We check in on their enthusiasm level with whatever they're doing."

We think Coach Humphreys's approach serves as a great guide for parents who are trying to decide whether their child should specialize in a sport. While we don't believe in kids calling all the shots, a child's enthusiasm, enjoyment, and passion are what make for a successful experience.

Strength and fitness

Multisport athletes also develop different groups of muscles that improve performance in other sports. They're using different motions, developing different muscle sets. The skill sets are different as well. Using new skills—as when a wrestler plays baseball, or when a volleyball player tries soccer—actually helps develop other ones.

I (Dave) wish my son Ryan had played volleyball. Because it uses different muscles, because it requires a different strategy, because it involves a different set of problem-solving skills,

I'm convinced that it would have made him a better basketball player. His footwork, body positioning, and eye-hand coordination would have improved.

What I find most fascinating is that college coaches—those for whom young players are aspiring to play, and those whom parents imagine as they make sports decisions with their kids—are encouraging reducing the amount of specialization. They're the ones encouraging kids to play more than one sport. But somehow the message isn't getting through. It is not the college coaches and athletics directors who are pressuring kids and parents in the single-sport specialization direction; it's the high school, club, and travel team coaches. Too often the coaches of our youngsters are more concerned about their own personal gain than that of our children. Most of them mean well, but they also must juggle other pressures and agendas.

I (Margot) grew up in Chicago when the Chicago Bears dominated the NFL (this may or may not have been true, I admit.) I have a distinct memory of running back Walter Payton wearing a tutu. It happened when the Bears squad was being trained in ballet to improve their performance on the gridiron. I also confess that my memory of the tutu may or may not be accurate. But seeing photos of the gargantuan Chicago Bears in a dance studio was equally jarring.

Ever since the Bears donned their ballet shoes, we've continued to see the benefits of multisport participation throughout the sporting world.

Each February, more than three hundred of the best college football players are invited to the NFL scouting combine in Indianapolis. Kristin Lantz, an athletic trainer who works with pre-combine athletes, notes that of the 350 football players who were invited to attend the most recent combine, 83 percent of them are multisport athletes.

The last shall be first

Remember Lisa? She was the captain of a team in a sport that wasn't her strongest. The value that came from that—from not specializing in one sport—was invaluable in shaping her into the intelligent, gifted woman she is today.

Will kids naturally choose to play those sports in which they're weaker? They might not. But as you consider encouraging your kids to play a variety of sports, remember that it's a good experience for kids to play on a team where they're not a star! It's good to learn what it's like to not be a starter. It's a bonus to discover a different role on a team. It's beneficial to learn from another type of coach. Admittedly, it's not glamorous, but this is how young people develop positive self-awareness.

Christian parents—those who purpose to pattern their lives after a guy who taught that we find our lives by losing them—don't need to be anxious that our children get ahead of others. Again, we're not talking about losing games on purpose or dropping buckets into our opponent's goal. We're describing the gift we've received that has set us free from bowing to the world's insistence that we scramble our way to the top. Our acceptance and even embrace of second place, or last place, models the Jesus way for our children.

Indoor, outdoor; hands, feet

I (Margot) had heard that playing multiple sports was better for kids than playing just one, and I asked Dave exactly why that was. So here's what it looks like . . .

My daughter, Zoe, plays volleyball in the fall and soccer in the spring. The two sports seem, at face value, to have little in common: one outdoor, one indoor; one using feet, one using hands; one that's a scramble of players from both teams, and one where players from opposing teams only brush against one another at the net. Yet both add value to Zoe's experience of the other.

Soccer is a possession game. Unlike that unwieldy amoeba of four-year-olds following a soccer ball, the player who's controlling the ball needs to be strategic about where it goes next. So setting up plays in volleyball is great preparation for this fundamental component of soccer. If Zoe learns to keep her eye on the ball, her head in the game, and an awareness of her peripheral vision in one sport, that carries over to the other. In both sports she's constantly aware of the two people she can pass to, since soccer often ends up being three on three. She learns how to move into position strategically. She learns when to leave space by taking a defender, or a spiker, with her. The footwork she develops in volleyball serves her in soccer; the spatial awareness and angles of play she develops in soccer help her in volleyball.

The carryover value between sports—even the most unlikely—benefits athletes in ways that aren't always calculable.

Well-rounded kids

National Hockey League alum Mark Messier is concerned about what he sees happening in youth hockey today. Messier, winner of six Stanley Cups, played twenty-five years in the NHL with the Edmonton Oilers, New York Rangers, and Vancouver Canucks. Messier, inducted into the Hockey Hall of Fame in his first year of eligibility, is considered to be one of the greatest NHL players ever.

He grieves the effect of so much money in minor sports—being paid by families and being received by leagues and personal coaches and trainers. (Soccer snobs, please note that the term *minor*, from the lips of this Canadian, doesn't mean "not as cool as soccer." It means kids!)

In an interview with Thousand Islands Youth Hockey, Messier's face and voice register deep concern over the state of youth sports. He lists several other concerns, in addition to money, explaining, "You gotta get the money out of minor sports . . . there's too much hockey being played, families are being broken up because of the travel, weekend tournaments."

Wait.

Did one of the best hockey players of all time say that there's "too much hockey being played"?

Yes. "Too much" is a real phenomenon in youth sports. Playing rigorously four seasons a year from the age of five doesn't engender a love of the game in kids. It produces burnout and dropout.

Messier notes that .007 percent of kids who play hockey make it to the NHL. "If your kid is in hockey to become an NHL player, you're missing what sports is really about. Sports is about the mental and physical and emotional well-being of the kids." He adds, "Youth sports have got to be about the life lessons that you're learning, the camaraderie, and the dressing room, and the way you can be good teammates."

Messier recognizes that early specialization is robbing children of what sports should be about. Age seven, he claims, is not an appropriate age to begin playing one sport year-round. Nor is ten. He even claims that age twelve is "young." Messier suggests age fourteen, offering, "At fourteen they're old enough to realize themselves exactly where they want to go."

Please hear that specializing in a sport by playing no other sports throughout the year isn't serving your seven-year-old, ten-year-old, or twelve-year-old. You love your kids well when you give them a chance to be well rounded.

Later specialization

We suspect that parents who don't share our concerns about the state of youth sports will have torn up this book or thrown it into the fireplace a few chapters ago. Like maybe in the first few sentences.

But if you're a parent who has questions about whether travel leagues and single-sport specialization are good for your child, let me (Dave), as a university athletics director, say that I don't have a one-size-fits-all answer for you. I do believe that that level of play does have its place. A lot of athletes want to improve their game during their junior or senior years of high school, especially if they're looking to play in college.

I respect that. I get it. And I think the junior and senior years of high school are a good time to commit to one sport, if that is their choice. I do know that it is extremely difficult to play more than one sport at the collegiate level, with the way the sports programs have developed.

What I'd like to encourage parents to avoid is plunging children who are too young into specialized, year-round sports. These children will likely end up getting injured or dropping out or burning out because they were pushed to specialize early.

I fear that too often the most well-meaning parents are operating on misleading information. Even really reasonable parents like Margot (she made me say that) have been conditioned to believe that if their children are to play for their middle school or high school teams, then they've got to start "keeping up" at age four!

My professional opinion about that?

It's a crock.

Yes, a number of kids who begin climbing the ladder probably will end up being strong players—if they're not one of those who drop out of the sport before high school. But there's no guarantee.

I want you to hear that your decisions don't need to be driven by fear.

LAZY, CHEAP, SENSIBLE

I (Margot) proudly identify as a "slacker mom." I won't say that we as parents have made all the right choices, but I will testify that our family has never felt overwhelmed by the commitments we chose for our three little athletes.

And that's no small thing.

Zoe is my oldest. She had an unsatisfying experience of "worship ballet" as a five-year-old—not at all worshipful—and played a few years of basketball with a church league and at the YMCA. She endured one very torturous year on a swim team, consistently placing last and watching her little brother come home with a fistful of ribbons. In middle school and high school, Zoe has played volleyball and soccer consistently and has played basketball intermittently. Today her body is healthy, and outside of the usual teenage drama, she's a happy camper.

Twenty-two months Zoe's junior is her brother Rollie, the lover of anything involving a ball. And then there's Abhi, eight months younger. Though neither Rollie nor Abhi has played in the rigorous competitive leagues available in our area, both have had the opportunity to represent their middle school teams: Abhi in soccer, and Rollie in soccer and baseball. Though some of the players who have played competitively year-round have developed more sophisticated skills, both of my boys are enjoying playing.

Today, as teens, Zoe, Rollie, and Abhi are all learning and growing and enjoying playing.

Sometimes people ask me, "Isn't it just crazy, with three teenagers? All the running around? Do you just live in your car?"

"Nope," I answer. "Not crazy."

That doesn't mean that tomorrow I won't be grabbing fast food between Rollie's baseball game and Zoe's soccer game. That will definitely happen. But our approach does mean that a few decades from now, my kids will have other memories of their childhood besides the inside of a minivan and the sidelines of a soccer field. They won't have nightmares about "that coach," and they might even still enjoy the game. That's my hope.

All of this goodness happened accidentally, because my husband and I were too lazy and too cheap to make more aggressive commitments to our children's athletic endeavors. And we did value a routine that usually let us eat dinners together at home and gave kids needed downtime on the weekends. It just turns out that lazy, cheap, and sensible was the magic trifecta that worked for our family.

STORIES OF EXCELLENCE THAT BELIE THE MYTH

If this slacker story did not inspire you to reconsider early specialization, consider these stories of excellence.

Jeff Hollenbach is a high school teacher and football coach in Pennsylvania. He was a quarterback at the University of Illinois and was invited to the Pittsburgh Steelers training camp. Jeff's son Sam grew up being very interested in playing football. Yet after witnessing the administration and coaching in the local peewee football organization, Jeff believed he could do more for Sam in the family's backyard. Though Sam no longer played with the local league, he went on to play at the University of Maryland and for the Washington Redskins.

Erik Kratz didn't start catching for his high school baseball team until his senior year. He wasn't heavily recruited by Division I and II schools and ended up playing at Eastern Mennonite University. Erik became a two-time Old Dominion Athletic Conference Player of the Year and holds the NCAA

Division III record for doubles in a career. He played for the Kansas City Royals in the 2014 World Series and is currently playing for the San Diego Padres.

Sam's family made a choice to not push him to specialize on year-round peewee teams when he was young. And Erik never even donned a catcher's mask until he was seventeen!

The research shows that if either of these guys had specialized early, playing all four seasons, they likely would have burned out before ever accomplishing all that they have.

John O'Sullivan is the author of *Changing the Game* and the founder of the Changing the Game Project, which serves families who are navigating the world of youth sports. O'Sullivan begs parents to educate themselves, explaining,

> The common mythology around youth sports that tells you to have your child specialize as soon as possible, focus on results instead of excellence, and that sports is an investment in a future scholarship have become conventional wisdom. But they are wrong; they are not based in science or psychology or coaching best practices. They are driven by people making money off of sports, and they are driven by parental fear of letting their kids down. Let the experience belong to your kids, help them find their passion instead of determining it for them, and they are far more likely to succeed in sport and life.

We treasure O'Sullivan's charge to parents. As you notice what's driving your choices—the opinions of people who will make a buck off you or the fear of letting your kids down—remember that your motivations, as a person of faith, won't necessarily be the same as those driving other parents and families.

You're not driven by fear, but by love.

Q&A with Margot

Question: My nine-year-old is begging me to play base-ball year-round. Help!

Answer: Some of the best parenting advice I ever received was "Say yes whenever possible."

Can the shower wait until morning? Yes. Can homework happen after the last four minutes of this show? Yes. Can I get my hair cut into a Mohawk? Yes.

I won't lie: none of those are *easy* yeses. But they do allow me to save the noes for when they're really needed.

I want to encourage you to be bold to use your no when it's appropriate. Notice what your gut is telling you and trust yourself to know when an opportunity that might be right for another child isn't right for yours.

If you have concerns that a particular athletic opportunity isn't best for your child—physically, emotionally, socially, spiritually—or for your family—due to excessive financial or time commitments—use your no. It's an important tool in the parenting toolbox. And although it's rarely popular, when used at the right time it is one way for you to love your child well.

Q&A with Dave

Question: When is the right time for travel and specialization?

Answer: I believe that participating in travel teams, if it makes sense for a child and for a family, should begin between ages twelve and fourteen. Prior to that, I believe there is greater potential for harm than good. Developmentally, your child will be better able to understand the implications of a commitment to this activity. And it's also about the time when, having experienced a broad scope of sporting opportunities, a child may begin to gravitate toward a particular sport.

Specialization in one sport, when a child chooses to do so, is appropriate to begin in either tenth or eleventh grade. While I still don't advocate playing any sport year-round—to protect a child's body—focusing on one sport toward the end of high school is reasonable. And by that time your athlete should begin to have an idea of whether a college sport is of interest, or possible. College coaches don't have to see an athlete play multiple times in the recruiting process, so playing in one or two showcase tournaments is normally sufficient to be seen and for college coaches to determine whether they're interested in recruiting a young person for their program.

Myth Four

There's No Harm in Participating in Youth Sports

Jessica, who works as a children's ministry director, is the married mom of three children. Joel, who's fifteen, plays baseball and basketball. Miranda, thirteen, played soccer until recently. And Serafina, eleven, is a dancer and a gymnast. Because Jessica's husband, Greg, works thirty minutes away from home, Jessica is in charge of much of the kids' transportation on weekdays.

For a few years before Serafina started gymnastics, Jessica could manage. Sometimes she'd need transportation help from a teammate's mom. Some days Joel would have to wait with her during Miranda's soccer practice. And sometimes Joel would be the last kid standing, coaches glancing at their watches, as

Jennifer skidded into the elementary school parking lot after snatching up Miranda from soccer.

But when Serafina began competitive gymnastics, Jessica and Greg's family life became almost unmanageable.

Like a lot of families, Jennifer's is stretched thin.

Whether she's barreling down the interstate toward the gym or mentally scheduling the afternoon while she's at work, Jessica experiences a chronic sense of frenzy. She always feels tired. She feels guilty for constantly dragging kids to their siblings' events. She feels bad that they're forced to do their homework in the car. She feels ashamed about how much food they eat from McDonald's. She feels growing anxiety with every check she writes for sports. She describes her life as feeling as if she's on a gerbil wheel.

In his TEDx talk, author John O'Sullivan calls this frantic pace "the race to nowhere." O'Sullivan sees kids dropping out of sports. He sees their relationship with their parents being damaged. He sees them bearing both physical and emotional scars.

Today families like Jennifer's are scrambling around that wheel to nowhere, constantly trying to get to the next level. If they're playing U12, they're trying to get to U14. If they're playing middle school, they need to get to high school. If they're playing in college, then after that—as I (Dave) remind recruits on my campus—it's church league slow-pitch softball!

Unfortunately, there are a lot of families like Jessica's on "the race to nowhere." They want to believe that the time and money and energy they have poured into their children's athletic endeavors are "worth it." They want to believe that everything they're doing is good for their children.

But when Jennifer wakes up at two in the morning, she isn't so sure.

By the time she was eleven, Serafina was battling repeated shoulder injuries. By twelve, Miranda was begging to drop out of soccer; she since has. And Jennifer has seen Joel suffer emotionally from his interactions with two particularly aggressive and derogatory coaches.

Is it worth it?

Lisa Delpy Neirotti is an associate professor of sports management at George Washington University. She is also the mom of a young lacrosse player, and she gets it. "You just want to give your kids the best, so if that means going onto this special soccer team and paying this coach, that is what you do," says Neirotti.

Parents begin with the best of intentions, but for many, the experience can spiral out of control. "It starts out that parents want their kids to play something just to be active," Neirotti says. "Then if they show talent, they are kind of put through the process. The coaches encourage the parents to go up a division and before you know it, you're on a travel team and you are sucked into it."

With the best of intentions, many families, like Jennifer's, have been sucked into a system that may not be as benign as we'd like to believe.

Children can be subjected to harm from overinvolvement in youth sports through participation in travel teams, showcase tournaments, early specialization, private coaching, year-round training, and similar efforts. The kinds of consequences we're describing aren't evident in kids who are engaged in sports in the neighborhood or in more casual rec leagues. So while we continue to believe that sports participation has numerous valuable benefits, we have concerns about what happens in much of organized youth sports culture: overuse injuries, burnout, loss of childhood, misperceptions about the true benefits of sport, and damaged relationships between children and parents.

Having a grumpy coach or icing a sore elbow doesn't top any parent's list of concerns that keep them up at night. In light of other dangers threatening children today—pornography, alcohol, drugs, predators—it's easy to reason about involvement in youth sports and wonder, "What's the harm?" But again and again we have seen the harm that comes to children subjected to overly aggressive involvement in youth sports. By exposing a few of these dangers, our hope is that you can protect your child from unnecessary harm.

BURNOUT

A young woman named Julie, nineteen, came into my (Dave's) office last week, at the end of the soccer season, to let me know she wouldn't be playing for our school the following year.

"I'm done," she announced.

I leaned back in my chair to listen.

"I've been playing since I was five. And since I was eight I've played all year long: practices every week, games every weekend. Every weekend we were driving someplace else for a game. Sometimes tournaments twice a month."

I'd met Julie's parents and I knew that they were, shall we say, *motivated*. Her dad had played soccer in college and had coached many of Julie's teams throughout the years.

"I get that all of that was to get me here, and I feel bad about it for my parents," Julie continued. "But I'm worn out. And I didn't realize how much of 'life' I've been missing. I just don't enjoy soccer anymore."

I've had a version of this conversation with young people more times than I care to count. Some, like Julie, are just burnt out. Others decide they no longer want to put their bodies through the punishing strain of injuries.

Another soccer player on campus recently confessed to me, "I would have quit in high school, but I knew that my parents would freak out."

A baseball player shared, "I've spent my entire life with this schedule. I've missed out on relationships and on other activities."

A pro golfer I know, whose dad had worked at a country club, told me, "I didn't have a childhood like you probably had. I wasted my childhood, although I did become a good golfer. I spent all my days at the golf course."

At some point, each of these players had his or her own wake-up call. For Julie, it was when she got to college and saw something different. "I got to school this year and saw people throwing a Frisbee on the quad. And I want to do that! Maybe kids did that in high school; I don't know. There are all these other things I want to do in life."

Julie no longer enjoyed soccer. Though she may have loved it at one point, it now felt like the enemy. It was what had been keeping her from life.

Because we do strive for our athletes to have a well-rounded college experience, I knew not all of the stress Julie was feeling was from our program. For the last eleven years she had missed sleepovers at friends' homes, youth group mission trips, and soccer playoffs for her own high school team—all because she'd been traveling around the region playing games and tournaments. I don't think I'm overstating it when I say that she'd missed a lot of her childhood. I've heard this from a number of athletes who have gotten caught up in the youth sports explosion.

A few years ago a young woman came to my college to play softball. She'd graduated from high school in June and arrived on campus in August. Between June 15 and August 15, she had played seventy softball games! It doesn't take a physical trainer to know that that can't be good for anyone. But I encounter it again and again.

Seeing more and more college athletes dropping out because they're burnt out breaks my heart as an athletics director. When a young person who once loved the game no longer does because he's been pushed beyond what's healthy, something has gone wrong.

Melissa Walsh, author of *The Rookie Hockey Mom*, sees a lot of dads pushing their kids hard in hockey. She observes, "These guys never played hockey. They really don't understand the players' experience. They push their kids into doing all these extras, as if youth hockey is a job, not a passion."

Walsh, with two decades of rink time under her belt, makes an educated guess about the results of this behavior. "I would bet that every one of these kids I've seen during my years at the rink who were harassed by their overzealous dads didn't make it through midgets-level hockey, for ages fifteen to eighteen." We suspect her guess is right on. She adds, "I saw many of these poor kids burn out before or during bantams, ages thirteen and fourteen."

Too often when athletes finally reach the goal that has been there since age five—to play college sports—they lose not only the passion but also the interest. While many of those who stop playing before their teen years simply don't enjoy it or don't have the skills to play, we wonder how many of them are already burnt out at age twelve after doing the same thing, sometimes year-round, for eight years.

High school teacher and coach Albert Zander has worked with some of the athletes that a college coach will likely never see. Lydia, a junior in high school, recently came to talk to him. She was anxious about telling her parents that she wasn't going out for volleyball. Instead, Lydia wanted to try cross-country, with her friends, for fun.

"She was worried," Coach Zander reports, "because her mom and dad had spent so much on travel volleyball, pushed her to the top teams, and were planning on visiting several colleges for volleyball. Her parents' plans were all in place—except their daughter's goals were never considered."

Zander saw the same thing recently with a hockey family who had spent countless weekends driving from their home near Chicago to Canada on weekends—only to have both of their kids stop playing in high school to play other sports for fun.

Zander, himself the father of five kids, recognizes that parents typically have the best of intentions. He notes, "I think at some point the kid liked the sport, maybe even loved it, and the parents tried to give their kid 'every opportunity to be successful' in that sport. This means joining the best travel teams, usually multiple teams, because the next best team is never the one they are on."

By the time they make it to high school, most kids who have specialized don't even have an interest in the sport. Coach Zander sometimes only discovers that some of the students in his physical education classes even played a sport outside of gym class when he hears other kids talking about how good the teen was in a sport he no longer plays. Additionally, some of the athletes who are feeling burnt out and are still playing ask Coach Zander to tell their parents that they're not going to play anymore.

He doesn't, but he helps them find the courage to do it.

Caution: Parents burning kids out

Because we believe in the power of sports to shape and develop children's bodies, minds, and hearts, we are disappointed when an adult hijacks the possibility of that experience for a child.

When Mindy was five, her athletic dad coached her peewee soccer team. One day he yelled in frustration, "This is supposed to be fun! If you don't want to be here, just come sit on the sidelines."

To his embarrassment, Mindy happily trotted right over to the sidelines and took a seat. It was the last year she played soccer.

Jack, fifteen, had been playing soccer competitively since he was four years old. Most of those years he'd played at least three seasons. Many weekends had been spent traveling to nearby cities for tournaments, and most weekdays were practice days.

When Jack tried out for his high school soccer team, he shone as one of the school's most talented players. After the second day of tryouts, the coach had made a preliminary cut, but on the third day Jack was still on the field. He knew there would be one more round of cuts before the final team was selected.

During the third-day tryouts, Jack lingered near the coach while the other players jogged off the field for a water break.

"Coach," Jack said quietly, "please cut me from the team."

Confused, the coach asked, "What? I don't think I understand."

Jack, head hung low, eyes on the field, explained, "My dad wants me to play, but I really don't want to. Can you just cut me?"

The coach mulled over Jack's request for a moment. Then he answered, "When I choose a team, I will choose the best players. That sounds like a conversation you need to have with your dad."

Jack, keenly aware of the conflict that conversation would cause with his dad, offered a reluctant "Okay, sorry."

In my years as an athletics director on a college campus, I (Dave) have seen more students like Jack than I wish I had.

Many of these students have, ostensibly, come to my school for the opportunity to play their sport. Yet I see so many who are completely burnt out from the rigors of playing so frequently throughout their childhoods. Too many have confided in me, "I would have quit last year, but I knew my dad couldn't deal with it."

In his TEDx talk, John O'Sullivan, who spent four years as a Division I men's soccer coach, reports that 70 percent of children drop out of organized sports by the age of thirteen. In other words, almost three-quarters of kids are done before high school. And O'Sullivan invites the audience to ask why.

To answer that, O'Sullivan describes a competitive ten-year-old boys' soccer game. A coach is screaming at his team and yanks a kid out of the game. Then the dad starts yelling.

"This," says O'Sullivan, "is exactly why kids drop out of sports."

O'Sullivan cites a study out of Michigan State University analyzing the reason that kids are quitting. The most frequently mentioned answers kids gave include:

"I'm tired of being criticized."

"I'm afraid to make mistakes."

"There's too much emphasis on winning."

Adults, by pushing their children to achieve, are robbing children of the joy of sports.

Caution: Coaches burning kids out

Sometimes parents are the problem, and other times coaches can push kids toward burnout. When Coach Zander warns parents about burnout, he shares his son's experience, explaining "My oldest son convinced me when he was in fifth grade to let him play youth football, way before I wanted him to."

Did you hear that? This coach knows what you're facing.

"Some of the coaching techniques my son experienced, and I observed, frequently confirmed my worst nightmares," Zander reports. "They challenged his fifth-grade manhood, did very little teaching of basic fundamentals, made it all about the x and o, ignored anyone new to the sport, and just sucked the confidence out of him."

It was hard for Coach Zander to watch what was happening to his son.

He offers, "He went into that season as football being his favorite sport and now will hardly even acknowledge it because [of] how it made him feel about himself. They crushed his confidence and love for the game."

When I (Margot) heard Coach Zander share about his son, I realized that it was exactly what had happened to my son several years before. In the intervening years since a horrible flag football half season, before the league crumbled, I had completely forgotten that my son Rollie had once loved football. But the league was so haphazard that there were just three teams. Which meant that every other game, Rollie's scrawny Bad News Bears football team, coached by a young but well-meaning coach, was matched against the New England Patriots. Practically. The opposing team, who'd been playing together for years, had custom NFL jerseys and pants, and Rollie's team had no uniforms at all, which only made the spectacle more painful to watch. After that nightmare experience, which was awful for me as a parent to watch, Rollie's love for the game quickly evaporated.

By the time an athlete reaches college—yes, a few actually do!—he is more developmentally ready to face a nasty coach. Or to navigate a system that seems unfair. At eight and nine and ten, though, our children don't have the emotional and physical resources to thrive in such pressing circumstances.

Coach Zander agrees. "Youth coaching is all volunteer, so it is mostly a crapshoot on what type of coaching they are getting at the youth level," he says. "The saddest part to us is the players we never see because they had a bad experience before we even get a chance with them."

The athletes who specialized early and come to me (Dave) are pretty exhausted by eighteen. A lot of them are tired of their bodies getting beaten up. I get that. Many of these students confess to me that they've been playing for all the wrong reasons all along. What concerns me most are the ones who say "I just don't love the sport anymore." While that's certainly a legitimate reason, we need to be asking why it's the case.

The why isn't a mystery. It's what Sandra's once baseball-loving son experienced, and it's what Coach Zander's son experienced: Excessive time commitment. Stress. Rejection. Little playing time. Bad coach.

WHEN KIDS AREN'T FREE TO BE KIDS

If you've ever seen five-year-olds play soccer, you've seen the amoeba. Wherever the ball goes, there are twenty-two little kids chasing after it! This is because they haven't yet developed spatial awareness.

Let's say it's Saturday morning and the amoeba is floating around the soccer field. Mom and Dad are sitting over there with their coffee mugs, yelling, "Spread out! Spread out!" If you're a soccer mom or dad, you have probably yelled the same thing.

The amoeba is migrating around the field when, all of a sudden, over the horizon, a whole series of helicopters flies into view. (This isn't a euphemism for helicopter parents. I'm talking about an actual fleet of cool flying vehicles in the sky.)

If you know five-year-olds, you know what happens. Forty-four little eyes are suddenly glued to the sky.

No, not quite. Forty-two eyes. Not Nick.

Nick has already been taught by his dad to take advantage of every opportunity the other team gives him. So he seizes the ball, dribbles through everyone else, and scores a goal. Nick runs back to the center of the field as proud as can be, yelling, "I scored! I scored!"

Incredulous, as the fleet of sky-birds slips out of sight, Ben, a member of the other team, answers, "Yeah, but you didn't see the helicopters!"

Because we've applied adult sports models to children's games, we're forcing Ben to develop a different relationship with Nick because Nick beat Ben, or because Nick's team is better than Ben's. We've interjected winning and losing into a game that would have just been fun in the backyard or on the playground.

That's a bit of what it looks like in soccer, and we suspect that you know exactly what it looks like in whatever sport your child plays.

The first problem in the story is that there are twenty-two players on the field. Soccer games for five-year-olds should never have eleven players on a team, and they shouldn't be playing on a regulation (adult) field with regulation (adult) goals.

The second problem is that parents and coaches are screaming at them, telling them to do something they are not capable of doing. It is like parents screaming at their five-year-old to finish the calculus problem. We wonder how parents would like having their supervisor at work yell at them to do something that they haven't been equipped to do.

And the third issue is that the kids care far less about the game than coaches and parents do. They simply want to have fun with friends, and they want to watch the cool helicopters overhead. And those are goals that cannot be tallied on any scoreboard.

Melissa Walsh recognizes the ill effects of this "adult-ification" phenomena in hockey. She pleads, "Especially when they're little, don't jump teams for wins records or rankings. Some coaches of little guys teach inappropriate systems or concepts that are designed to be applied by higher-level players in certain situations, such as playing a trap to hold a lead." Walsh sees what is lost when this happens. She explains:

> When little kids play these concepts and systems inappropriately, what's sacrificed are the good habits kid hockey players should be developing when they're little, like carrying the puck through traffic. When kids are developing good long-term hockey-playing habits, they'll likely take many game losses in the short-term of their youth hockey career. Age-appropriate hockey is development- and fun-appropriate, not based on a team's win-loss ratio.

Walsh implores, "Fun first. Treat kid hockey players like kids. Too many in this sport are treating kids like adults."

If nothing seems alarming about Nick and Ben's soccer game, or the state of peewee hockey, it's because so many of us have come to take for granted the way that youth sports have evolved over the last few decades. We're blind to the multiplicity of ways we've simply applied adult sports models to children's recreation. We can't always fault the well-meaning adults. It's simply that we can't think through and with the eyes of a child. It has been too long since we were children ourselves.

One of the dangers of club sport programs is that too often the leaders (coaches and administrators) are not educators. So they do the only thing they know: adult sports. And for whatever reason, many of us have this strange desire for our kids to grow up too fast. And in the process, we are robbing them of their childhood.

Here are a few of the ways that adults apply adult models to kids' sports:

- *Drafts.* At tryouts, your child throws and catches the ball a few times with another kid, and then some adults who are watching decide if they want your kid on their team. So before the season even starts, there is pressure to perform in front of adults to see if a child is good enough.

- *Leagues.* We model our youth sports after the professional sports. We dress kids in uniforms with sponsors' names on the back and give them team names like Pistons, Celtics, Reds, or Orioles. We seem to want to make professionals out of ten-year-olds. The reality is that no matter how you dress them, no matter what you call them, and no matter how you organize your league, ten-year-olds will still play like ten-year-olds.

- *All-star teams.* We have never understood what anyone gains when two communities choose their "best" players to see who is better at six-year-old basketball—using ten-foot baskets!

- *Tournaments.* Tournaments place major emphasis on games and less on the importance of practice.

- *Youth leagues as a "farm system" for high school sports.* In some communities, unless you play for a certain club team, you probably won't make the high school team.

- *Limited playing time for most.* Many times, the coach's son is the best player on the team and is either the shortstop or the pitcher. Everyone should be given the opportunity to try any position he or she wants, at least in practice, and everyone should experience sitting on the bench.

- *Competition before children are developmentally ready.* Scores and league standings force children to compete against friends too early. Changing teams every week would reduce the significance of the result of competition and its influence on the game.

- *Plays organized beyond the cognitive development of children.* The results orientation of leagues forces coaches to develop plays and teach strategy instead of focusing on the development of basic skills. They are asking kids to do things they aren't capable of.

- *League politics.* Similar to situations in the corporate adult world, in youth sports it might not be as much who you *are* as who you *know*. Some coaches will do anything to win.

- *Scoreboards.* Scoreboards change the purpose of the game from enjoying fun and friends to tallying who wins. It is an added pressure kids don't need.

Those are all adult systems. When kids organize their own sports, they use the logic that kids use. Here's what it looked like in my neighborhood when I (Dave) was growing up: Ball games in the backyard lasted until dark. We stood in whatever area we thought the batter would hit the ball. We played "shirts and skins" or borrowed white T-shirts from the house where we were playing. We changed teams every time we played. We made up rules to fit the occasion or changed the rules to fit the game we were playing. Unfortunately, adults have too often forgotten how to think like children, and we organize children's lives the way professionals have organized those of adult athletes—even when it isn't always in the best interest of the kids.

EXTRINSIC AND INTRINSIC VALUES

When Pittsburgh Steelers linebacker James Harrison discovered his sons had been awarded participation trophies for completing a season in the local athletic league, he posted on Instagram: "These trophies will be given back until they EARN a real trophy." He added, "I'm not about to raise two boys to be men by making them believe that they are entitled to something just because they tried their best . . . cause sometimes your best is not enough, and that should drive you to want to do better."

What Harrison was describing was the difference between extrinsic motivation and intrinsic motivation. This concept speaks to internal and external incentives. For example, people may watch their diets and exercise because they value good health (intrinsic), and if they look a little leaner in the process, that's fine too (extrinsic). Like their adult counterparts, kids are also motivated by intrinsic and extrinsic rewards.

Within competitive youth sports, some of the external rewards include new uniforms, big trophies, staying at hotels, eating out at restaurants, practicing less, and playing in more games. Intrinsic rewards, on the other hand, include a love of the game, a desire to improve, wanting to be part of a team, and willingness to sacrifice for the team. While we're all motivated by both types of rewards, which ones lead to the kinds of lasting values that you want to develop in your children? We'd wager a guess that you, like us and like many other Christian parents, are purposing to instill intrinsic values like community, sacrifice, and hard work.

So it's important to know that most psychologists agree that the introduction of extrinsic values too early in life inhibits the development of intrinsic values.

Let that sink in for a minute. *Extrinsic values inhibit growth of intrinsic values.*

Is it possible that the glitz and glamour of the travel teams, showcases, all-star games, and other extrinsic rewards are one of the reasons our children are burning out? A focus on these extrinsic rewards doesn't allow intrinsic values to be developed. Does the reason that Joshua or Madeline "really loves soccer" have to do with the kinds of values that provide immediate gratification, or with a real love for the game?

One of the reasons I (Dave) have always believed that student athletes at Division III institutions—the ones whose games will never be televised on ESPN, who won't receive hefty scholarships, and whose jerseys aren't licensed to big manufacturers—are playing for all the right reasons is that, without any of the perks, they possess the three attributes any college player needs to succeed: a love of the game, the desire to get better, and the willingness to sacrifice for the team.

So it's actually very predictable that when some student athletes reach the collegiate level where those extrinsic rewards aren't offered, and they haven't developed the requisite intrinsic values, they stop playing. That observation isn't an indictment of young athletes as much as it is of the system we've created. The fact that this is how high school, college, and professional sports are all organized doesn't mean it's what's best for children, adolescents, and young adults. One poll reveals that the number one reason given by children for quitting sports is lack of fun. When it's no longer fun, they no longer want to do it. The kids who may have jumped into sports to have fun discover that, in many leagues, fun isn't as important as a first-place trophy.

Many parents we speak with retort, "Well, we have to learn how to win and lose. That's part of life." And while we agree, we don't think kids have to do it in kindergarten. Children will still get the benefit if that lesson is learned later. The harm we've done with these adult sports models is that we've taken the fun

Five qualities of a successful, motivated athlete

1. She loves the game.
2. He desires to improve.
3. She is willing to sacrifice for the team.
4. He accepts his role on the team.
5. She understands how to improve.

out of the sport. In doing so, we've robbed many children of the enjoyment of sports and the joys of their childhood. We've conditioned them to play for extrinsic rewards.

At the University of Southern California, with a click of a mouse, prospective student athletes can preview full-sized photos of the various gear and uniforms that will be provided to them when they sign on. But it's not just Division I athletes who expect rewards. I (Dave) recently heard from my own university's baseball coach that a fairly common question he hears from recruits early in the recruiting process is, "Are you a Nike or Under Armour program? And a routine second question is, "Where do you go to play during spring break: California or Florida?" These student athletes are asking about the "perks" of the various programs they're visiting. By the time they reach the collegiate level, they've already been conditioned to *expect* extrinsic rewards, and those rewards greatly influence their college choice.

One shining exception to this rule was a female athlete I recently learned about from a colleague at a Division III school in

Pennsylvania. Like my university, it is also a Christian school. When this young woman chose not to attend a Division II school where she'd received an offer for a basketball scholarship, her parents refused to pay for her education. She had chosen a school that was the right educational, social, and spiritual choice for her, without any promise of extrinsic rewards from the school, and her parents penalized her for the decision.

READING A CHILD'S CUES

Kids are geniuses when it comes to sensing what their parents want. Feeling the pressure of pleasing parents along with the pressure to win can be too much for some kids.

My (Dave's) son Derek played Little League baseball in Halifax, Pennsylvania, during the years that I was a director at a Christian camp. In his first year of transitioning from hitting off the tee in T-ball to having the ball pitched by a player from the other team, he started out very well. But about a third of the way through the season, he started struggling to hit the ball. I could see that he was becoming less confident and a bit anxious every time it was his turn to bat.

Wearing a wobbly batting helmet one size too big, Derek cautiously approached the plate. When he positioned himself on the outside edge of the batter's box, the coach motioned for him to move closer to the plate. Hesitantly, Derek moved a bit closer.

The pitcher wound up and put one right over the plate. A perfect pitch. Derek watched the ball slide past him.

"STRIKE ONE!" the umpire called out.

"That's okay," his coach yelled. "Keep your eye on the ball. You did it before, you can do it again. You'll get the next one."

Derek halfheartedly positioned his bat for a swing. The second pitch, high and outside, was a ball.

"BALL!" the ump called.

Derek felt relieved. If he could just get three more of those, he'd be in business. The next pitch floated right over the plate.

Statuelike, Derek watched the ball pass and immediately looked at the ump.

"STRIKE TWO!"

"That's okay!" his coach yelled. "But you gotta swing. If it's a good one, take a swing at it."

The final pitch was a bit low, but the ump called it a strike.

As he turned to look at the ump, Derek's disappointed expression suggested that blame for the strikeout fell on the umpire. Heading back to the bench, he felt relief that he was no longer at bat.

Being a firstborn child who was compliant and wanting to please, Derek wasn't ready, at age nine, to deal effectively with failure—especially since he had been successful earlier in the season. It was much easier to blame the ump than to admit and deal with his own failure.

We're not saying that every kid who's nervous to swing isn't emotionally ready to deal with failure, but we are saying that

Best comment to share with your child after a game

"I like watching you play."

(Best to reserve this one for a game when your child gets playing time. Otherwise . . . awkward.)

attentive parents can notice cues that their children are sending in high-pressure situations and can offer safe spaces to talk about it.

When parents aren't able to recognize cues from their children about how they are feeling about playing—sometimes for years on end—they cause them more frustration than is necessary.

RETURNING TO A MORE KID-FRIENDLY MODEL

Last year Mindy and Alex signed up their nine-year-old son, Allan, for Little League.

Beyond the name, though, there was nothing "little" about it.

For this active young family, traveling to and from the baseball fields felt big—there was typically one practice and three games a week. The other boys who'd been playing since age five felt big. The fierce competition and the intensity of the parents in the bleachers felt big. And the cost of registration and equipment definitely felt big.

By the end of the season, Mindy and Alex were exhausted and decided they needed to do something a little differently. Allan had spent most games just standing around, and maybe got to bat two times. And because the number of games had so outweighed the number of practices, their son hadn't really gained much skill as a player.

Allan's dad is a mathematician. And when Allan's parents did the math, the couple realized that if they committed just the time they'd spent in the minivan last season to playing baseball with him in the backyard, he'd have a better chance of improving than he did on his Little League team. The time together as a family would be an added bonus.

In the time since Allan has been liberated from the minivan, something has happened that neither Mindy nor Alex had anticipated. Allan lives a few blocks from school and has begun hanging around there to play pickup games with his friends.

Mindy raves, "He is gaining so much more. He's playing more often. He's had to develop competencies and independence. There are no coaches yelling at him."

What Mindy sees happening socially is a win as well. "Parents don't interfere at all," she explains. "Kids manage the whole process. They figure it out. It's been great for him."

Play.

It's what kids do.

AN ORGANIZATIONAL WIN

Motivated parents and coaches who aren't lucky enough to live in Mindy's neighborhood can create other great alternatives for kids. When I (Dave) lived in Lancaster, Pennsylvania, I started a Saturday morning basketball clinic. Families paid a couple of bucks and kids showed up to learn skills.

We never turned the scoreboard on.

We never handed out uniforms.

Everybody had the same colored shirt.

Each week, after we'd worked on skills, we'd play a game. And each week we'd divide up teams differently. The kids loved playing, but there were two differences between our clinic and other local leagues: they weren't wearing jerseys in contrasting colors—except pinnies to identify teammates!—and there was no scoreboard tallying baskets.

The program ran for eight weeks, and not once did a parent stay to watch. Not one. Now, had I turned the scoreboard on, it would have been a different story. Had I given the team a name and challenged a team in another league to a match, parents would have shown up.

When parents picked up their kids at noon on Saturdays, most greeted their kids with the question, "Did you have fun today?" When there are uniforms and scoreboards, "Did you have fun?" ceases to be the inquiry. Instead, parents press:

"Why'd the coach put you there?"

"I think you should have . . ."

"Let's go home and work on . . ."

Without the shirts and the scoreboard:

"Did you have fun?"

"What did you enjoy most?"

"What happened?"

For a lot of parents, those are the questions they ask their four- or five-year-olds after a Saturday morning soccer game— the kind where every player on the field just chases the ball around in a big swarm. We encourage you to hang on to the spirit you had when your child was four or five and pitch these open-ended questions to your older athletes as well. Parents have incredible influence to shape a child's athletic experiences.

WHERE'S THE HARM?

The reason I (Dave) remain in sports administration is that I believe in the great potential of sports to develop character and resilience in children, teens, and young adults. But I certainly do not believe that signing a registration form for a travel team, or entrusting a child to an adult the high school has found to coach a team, means that children will have a great experience of sports.

I've seen too much harm children and families have endured as a result of our current youth sports culture.

Families are struggling, their dollars and hours stretched to the breaking point. As a result of negative experiences, children are burning out and dropping out of sports. Those who continue at a pace and intensity too rigorous for children are suffering from overuse injuries and damaged family relationships. They're missing some of the important experiences of childhood as they're bullied by adult sports models that just aren't always appropriate for kids.

And yet, even as we survey this dismal landscape facing families and kids today, we have hope that we can offer something different for our children. We are inspired when we see parents like Mindy and Alex, who offered their son a different path to enjoyment of sports. We're buoyed when we hear of leagues that are teaching skills and growing kids. We're encouraged by dads and moms who want to preserve their children's bodies from overuse at young ages. And we absolutely love to see great coaches who are committed to keeping the game fun for children.

We do believe that children can be harmed by youth sports. But we also believe in the inherent capacity of sports to help children grow and develop—when adults protect our kids and help create the kind of experiences that truly serve them.

Q&A with Margot

Question: Isn't it a little extreme to call youth sports "harmful"?

Answer: Yes and no.

If acknowledging the potential for harm in youth sports means throwing the sports-baby out with the sweat-filled bathwater by keeping kids home on couches, then that would be extreme.

As a mom in the trenches, I'm grateful for the cautions from an athletics director like Dave who knows so much about the physical, social, and emotional risks kids can face—and hopefully avoid!—in today's youth sports culture. Facing squarely the risks inherent in organized youth sports doesn't mean that I'll pull my kids from the beneficial athletic activities they enjoy. It does mean that I'll pay closer attention to the ways they're using and caring for their bodies. It means I'll help them carve out time for neighborhood friendships; I'll notice the ways coaches are engaging with my kids; and I'll speak with my children about their experience in helpful ways.

Understanding and facing the potential for harm is what allows me to best love my kids.

Q&A with Dave

Question: When is the right time for drafts, leagues, and other organized aspects of sport?

Answer:

Drafts. I don't think drafts are necessary at all—especially the kind where one kid at a time performs for adults and teams are made from that event. I suggest gathering all the kids together and playing a game in which everyone gets to play for equal amounts of time. The adults watch and then work together to divide up the teams so they are fairly even.

Leagues. Junior high is probably a good time to put an emphasis on leagues. You could have leagues in the earlier years as long as standings aren't kept and posted. Too many kids at those younger ages aren't equipped to deal with being on top or on bottom (and neither are most parents!). School teams belong to leagues, but I still oppose publicizing standings until high school.

Playing time. I support situations in which everyone gets to play every position—from coaching first or third base to sitting on the bench. Normally, at about ages twelve to fourteen, players begin to demonstrate tendencies and abilities that will help a coach decide where they might be most successful. Remember that few college athletes are playing the position they played in middle school or high school. The emphasis should be on learning the fundamentals of the game, not on learning a position.

Scoreboards. My belief is that no game needs a scoreboard until middle school. I know that sounds fanatical, but the reality is that plenty of parents (and players) know the score. There are far too many lopsided scores in youth sports to put them on display for everyone. Scores emblazoned on a scoreboard become a distraction and probably cause some kids to give up early in the game.

All-star teams. The Little League organization in baseball basically requires the selection of a team to represent their local league or community in an international tournament ending with the Little League World Series. I'm comfortable with this type of situation, although adult egos and politics can still harm kids in this tournament as well. (For example, in 2014, a Little League team from Chicago lost its United States championship title when it was discovered that the coaches had knowingly used players who lived outside of the team's area boundaries.) But in general, I'm okay with the Little League World Series, which is for eleven- and twelve-year-olds. What I'm uncomfortable with is a recreational league for eight-year-olds choosing an all-star team to play against a group of eight-year-olds from a neighboring town. I don't think terms like *all-star*, *elite*, and *premier* should be used in youth sports.

Myth Five

Youth Sports Instill Our Family's Values

Laurie and Eric are the parents of three boys, ages eight, eleven, and thirteen. All three guys are athletic and enjoy sports. The boys, by their own admission, are also a little bit addicted to video games. During the school year, Laurie and Eric limit the boys' screen time, but it often feels like an overwhelming task to monitor the boys' minutes. During school vacations, it's worse.

Laurie says that being their parent feels like being a nurse who's been charged with monitoring the crack consumption of cocaine addicts. The couple has experimented with unplugging their boys altogether, using timers, using online monitors, and employing an exchange in which boys can cash in minutes spent playing outdoors for screen minutes. Still, Laurie and Eric usually feel like they're failing miserably to help their boys be well-rounded people. They've actually paid them to walk six blocks to McDonald's and eat junk food. It's that bad.

Between the three boys, throughout the year, the family is involved in swimming, soccer, baseball, and basketball. And while Laurie and Eric aren't thrilled about the time, money, or miles on the minivan, they count any time that their boys are not glued to screens as a win. Compared to the FIFA 15 and Madden digital sporting experiences that turn their boys into mannequin zombies, and compared to the Big Mac bribery, participation in actual healthy, physical activity sounds great.

The boys are breathing fresh air and soaking in sunshine.

They're getting cardiovascular benefits.

They're engaging with other children. (Yes, their conversations with their friends do revolve mostly around the digital world, but at least they're speaking face-to-face, not by text.)

Though they're not entirely convinced, Eric and Laurie want to believe that through athletics their boys are learning about discipline and commitment and perseverance and all the other inspiring words on sports posters and TV ads for athletic shoes.

Eric and Laurie want to believe that organized youth sports are reinforcing the values they hold for their children.

QUESTIONABLE VALUES

Though sports have great potential to help your child grow further into the image of God and into mature, compassionate adults, inherent in today's youth sports culture is also the likelihood that—unexamined—your child's experience of sports might ingrain values to which you do not ascribe.

Loss of community bonds

As our culture has become more transient, with children crossing the country to go to college and families relocating for jobs, many of our relationships have become fragmented. This fragmentation is mirrored, today, in youth sports. While student athletes' primary commitment to a team used to be to their school's team, that is no longer the case. Today many players are choosing to forsake their school teams for elite teams. In many cases, the elite teams require them to.

There are tens of thousands of travel teams in Georgia and Florida alone, according to an estimate from the Atlanta-based Youth Amateur Travel Sports Association (YATSA). In 2000, a dozen teams participated in the first All-American Wood Bat Classic tournament in Atlanta; in 2014, nearly one hundred squads from half a dozen states participated. As YATSA executive director Rebecca Davis points out, "The fast growth absolutely blindsided us. Those days of rec ball and local Little League, or just going to the park and playing ball—those days are nonexistent. They're gone. Now it's all about travel."

While strong relationships can be built on travel teams, the setting doesn't afford the same kinds of opportunities to develop and deepen friendships as sharing life "on the ground" might. Members of school teams share the whole day together. They experience the same lunch menu, school assemblies, and daily practices. Members of travel teams typically get together for one or two practices and then spend the weekend at a tournament. The focus of travel team ball in the older childhood years shifts to the exposure of players to college coaches. Too often the special bonds of friendship that have developed in neighborhoods and churches, through years of going to school and playing together, are dropped for the individualism of the travel team culture.

David Mendell, a freelance writer and former reporter for the *Chicago Tribune*, sums up this emerging phenomenon in a recent column in the *Washington Post*: "Travel ball is not new—it's been around for a couple of decades. But participation in full-time travel baseball has exploded in recent years. . . . With the loss of so many players and their families to travel teams, our community leagues have lost a certain sense of community."

Detachment from faith community

Competitive youth sports are also pulling families away from their houses of worship. High school coach Albert Zander observes, "Nothing is sacred anymore, and Sunday has become tournament day." He adds, "I've observed long enough to see that the kid grows up and has no faith of their own because the message was communicated to them through the family's actions that sports are more important than their church, faith, or God."

As a college athletics director, I (Dave) have seen this on the other end. Parents who have driven their children from tournament to tournament, weekend after weekend, year after year, become distraught when their child goes to college and leaves the faith behind. Yet for years the parents have been communicating to the child that their faith community, communal worship, and church life aren't important. Parents rarely intend to communicate that, and following Christ might be very important to the parents themselves. Regardless, they have sent a clear message to their children that their faith community is not more important than their athletic schedule.

John is a good friend of mine who pastored a medium-sized church in Pennsylvania for several years. One fall, a couple came to see John about their son, who had just graduated from high school and wasn't planning to go to college right away.

These parents were concerned that their son wasn't involved in church or even showing interest in attending church events. They wondered if John had ideas for how they might get their son more interested in church, and they hoped that John and the leadership team might even intervene.

Never one to mince words, John reported that he wasn't surprised by their son's lack of interest in church. "I remember when your son was between the ages of ten and fourteen," John told them. "Your family missed a lot of Sundays and other church events as you took him all over the state and beyond with his travel team. You sent him a very clear message that church wasn't important. So I'm not surprised. And now you want me to fix it?"

I'm glad to report that, somehow, my friend John kept his job as a pastor!

Another pastor tells us that she considers the greatest "enemy" of her pastoral ministry these days to be travel teams. So many families prioritize their children's athletic commitments over their commitments to their church family that pastors, youth leaders, and other church leaders can feel like they're fighting a losing battle to keep church life vibrant and central in the lives of their parishioners.

That being said, we don't want to reduce the conversation about youth sports and faith to a formulaic question of whether a child misses church to play a game. That's very simplistic, and it doesn't help families. Too often we make the conversation about youth sports and church into a value judgment between a particular practice or game and a church event. Faith formation in our children happens all the time—yes, it happens on Sunday morning and Wednesday night, but also on Monday afternoon and Thursday evening and Saturday morning. Arguing about church attendance can cause us to miss the point. It is the cumulative effect and decisions about sports and church involvements that communicate to children what we value and what we hope they will value.

The barrage of scheduling decisions parents face for one or more children is a complicated equation! And it's one of the reasons we encourage families to dialogue before registering for a team. Sit down with a practice and game schedule the day the coach sends it home. Let the coach know right away which games or practices your child will miss because of the commitments—to church, to family, to others—that you already hold.

This is a conversation that has to your child. There may be reasons that your family does decide to forfeit an occasional Sunday worship, or Wednesday church supper, to accommodate your child's athletic schedule. But if you never loop your children in on your processings, or the logic you've used to make your choices, they could understandably assume that whatever you've opted *against* has less value than what you've opted *for*.

Endorsement of the macho ideal

It is the third game of the week for the Orioles—ten-year-olds, not pros—and Chad is pitching. Due to regulations limiting the number of pitches that players can throw, the team's strongest pitchers have all been "used up." Chad, without much pitching experience at all, is struggling on the mound. He's walked his third batter when the Nationals' biggest slugger steps up to the plate.

Chad is visibly upset, biting his lip to keep from crying. The coach asks the ump for a time-out and walks over to Chad. Chad's mom prays that the coach will put his arm around Chad, let him know that he thought Chad did his best, and then pat him on the back before sending him off to right field. Everyone on both benches would clap politely and breathe a deep sigh of relief.

But that's not what happens. Chad's coach doesn't put his arm around Chad. He doesn't bend down to speak gently with him at eye level. Chad's coach gives him a pep talk and, before walking away, barks, "Come on now, you can't cry over things like this. Get your game face on and get back in the game!"

Chad makes it through the traumatic inning, but dissolves into tears as the Orioles leave the field. He silently vows it will never happen again.

Too often sports promote a macho ideal, which scorns any show of weakness or emotion. While machismo may have been useful for survival, perhaps back in the days of cavemen, today most recognize that it's not useful for men, women, boys, or girls. And yet the "suck it up" culture of sports forces children, especially boys, to "armor up" emotionally to survive on the diamond, the gridiron, the court, or the field.

One emotion is allowed: anger. The explosive, aggressive emotion, fueling adrenaline in a way that probably did serve primitive humans well, is the single emotion tolerated in sports. Other "negative" emotions, though, are disallowed. Because most sports have historically been male-dominated, the unspoken rule denying children the freedom to show fear or sadness has been taught to boys for generations. As sporting opportunities for girls have increased during the last four or five decades, the macho rules have been communicated to them as well, loud and clear: displaying sadness or fear is a sign of weakness. If a girl keeper allows a goal, if a gymnast drops off the beam, if a cross country runner misses the gold by less than a second, the unspoken rule she has internalized is to hide emotion.

Tragically, the denial of emotion that athletes are taught is ritualized, in some high school and college-level sports, through brutal hazing. The humiliations to which the senior members of a team subject rookies are rooted in the macho ideal that permeates all levels of athletics. Such rituals establish dominance and galvanize, in their victims, a refusal to display weakness or emotion.

Parents, though, know that showing sadness or fear is actually a sign of being human. We're also aware that our kids will inevitably deal with coaches, officials, players, and players' parents who will say things like "Get your game face on and get back in the game!"

When Chad slides into his family's minivan after the game, his parents can respond in one of two ways. They might say something like, "I didn't like what I saw out there. You looked like you were about to cry in front of everyone. Don't be a baby—it's just a game. Man up. I don't want to see that again."

Or they might say, "I didn't like what I saw out there. I didn't agree when that coach told you it wasn't something to cry over. That was a really stressful situation that you weren't prepared for. Sure, I can understand why you might not have wanted to cry on the mound, but if there's any left in you, you can let it out now. It makes sense that you're sad."

The machismo of sports culture may not align with your family's values, and it may require parents to be intentional about creating space for healthy emotional development.

Demonstration of poor behavior

Study after study has proven that parents have more of an impact on their children's values and choices than we realize. Although, as they approach adolescence, our young children will eventually turn their gaze toward peers for the esteem and approval they once sought from us, parents remain the most significant influence in children's lives. Some of the values we want them to live into we've communicated verbally. We've told our children what we value, and we've outlined the ways we expect them to behave. Other values they've picked up from observation.

They've seen the kind of people we spend time with.

They've noticed the ways we spend our money.

They've watched the way we use our free time; whether we serve ourselves or serve the needs of others.

And even when they're on the field, the diamond, the grid-iron, the ice, the mats, or the bench, they watch and listen to the ways we behave at athletic competitions. Specifically, they notice the ways we behave toward players, coaches, and officials.

This summer, I (Dave) observed a basketball team camp for high school students that was also being used as a clinic for officials. Veteran Division I officials were providing education to newer officials to teach proper positioning and mechanics. Despite the fact that the setup was clearly a training ground for both players and officials, parents still blasted the refs from the sidelines and even from a running track above the courts! I thought I had already seen every manner of bad behavior from parents. But these who had the audacity to yell at a Division I ref during a summer league camp took the cake.

What these parents, and others like them, communicate to children in these encounters is that it's acceptable to be arrogant, rude, and disrespectful toward those in authority. On the other hand, parents who behave graciously toward officials, coaches, and players equip children with the kind of attitudes—humility, compassion, kindness, and understanding—that will serve them throughout the rest of their lives.

Loss of quality family time

We are also concerned about what we as parents communicate to our children when we designate youth sports activities—the entire family driving three hours to sit through three soccer games, for example—as "family time."

If we're honest, it's "sit in a van and sit on bleachers to watch one person perform" time. Outside of a middle schooler begging her father not to yell at the officials, there is often little interaction between family members. It's four people watching one person perform and then evaluating it afterward. We get frustrated when families tell us that going to the game is their family time. It is not. It's four people watching one person perform. That's not true family time.

We encourage families to take seasonal breaks from their child's sport. You'll have a hard time convincing us that, if you're playing soccer in the fall and spring, skipping those six indoor practice sessions or six indoor games in the winter will make a difference in an athlete's play.

Skip some games and practices and say to your son or daughter, "Hey, we're going to take a break this winter. Instead of going to the indoor training facility on Tuesday nights, we're going to invite another family over for dinner and we're going to play games." Or, "We're going to go to the soup kitchen and serve there for a couple of weeks."

Now those things? *Those* give you true family time.

And Christian families can be more intentional about the time they do give to youth sports. One of the rationales we hear from Christian families who are forfeiting Sunday worship for the sake of travel leagues is that they can "impact" or "reach" other families. While the intention is a good one, too often the implementation is weak.

If the goal is to reach out to other children and families, why do so many of us all hop in our minivans and drive the three hours to the tournament alone? If sports take you and your kids out of town on weekends, consider seizing opportunities to love and serve families right where you are. Offer to take a player under your wing for the weekend so his family can stay home and support other kids. Reach out to a team family who's hurting by taking them meals or providing childcare. Serve a family in economic crisis by secretly slipping the coach a check for their child's gear. Invite another family to attend a church potluck in the off-season.

Homogeneous environments and economic disparity

As a young child, Hunter would bounce a basketball around the block for an entire Saturday morning, practicing his dribbling. His family couldn't afford a backboard, but whenever he had the opportunity—at school or in a neighborhood recreational league—he was playing hoops. His rec league coach has confirmed that Hunter had a lot of talent. Hunter was determined to play basketball in middle school and high school. And, like many boys, he even dreamed of going pro.

The reality that unfolded during Hunter's school years was very different. In seventh grade, Hunter, a very smart boy, was falling behind in his classes. When his mother investigated, she discovered that it was because he lacked certain required notebooks needed for journaling and other assignments. He hadn't asked her to buy them because he was concerned about money. Hunter was ineligible to play basketball in seventh grade because of his failing grades. In eighth grade, he did not have a current physical on file with the school. His mother worked two jobs and had been unable to schedule an appointment before tryouts. Hunter didn't play.

Because he continued to improve and gain skills in his rec league, Hunter still hoped to play for his high school, which had the best basketball team in the city. When conditioning began, Hunter was unable to attend. He lived five miles from school and didn't have transportation to and from school other than the school bus. Although he wasn't able to attend conditioning regularly, he was able to attend tryouts. He did not make the team.

Hunter's rec league coach, Coach Mel, believes that Hunter is a more gifted player than 90 percent of the boys who made the team. The coaches, though, already knew the other players from AAU teams. They didn't know Hunter. Coach Mel also believes that missing conditioning hurt Hunter's chances of making the team.

Hunter's experience isn't atypical for children whose families have limited economic means. In fact, research shows that children in families making less than $35,000 per year begin organized sports almost two years later than children in families making more than $100,000 per year.

We don't believe that families who sign their children up for youth sports intend to self-select a fairly homogeneous environment for their children. But for families who value diversity, who believe that all children deserve opportunities for growth, this disparity becomes one more place where youth sports may not truly reflect a family's values.

WORTHY VALUES THAT CAN BE DEVELOPED IN YOUTH SPORTS

If we agree that parents can't assume that the values they hold will be reinforced in youth sports—priorities like community, church involvement, emotional health, family time, and diversity—we might also agree that there are important values that youth sports *can* develop in children. Let's look at four fundamental ones.

Identify your family's values

Many families haven't paused to identify the values they claim to hold, or dared to distinguish those from the ones they actually practice! Carve out some time to name the values you want to guide your life together.

1. Consider your values

Invite children to suggest the values that they think are important. You might help them understand values as "the way we want to live." Give them examples such as helping others, truth telling, working hard, sharing what we have, honoring God, loving people. (If you have very young children, this step of the exercise can be left to parents.)

Invite older children and adults to identify the core values espoused by your faith tradition. Then try to identify the ones you actually practice. (This might sting!)

2. Identify your values

Choose one, two, or three guiding values for your family and post them on the fridge.

3. Live according to your values

Ask yourselves when you see that list, do these values inform our family's experience of sports? (The connection may not be immediately evident; it may be revealed as opportunities unfold!)

Self-awareness

The first is self-awareness. When children compare themselves to other players—discovering their role on the team, identifying their strengths and weaknesses, learning whether they're a big fish in the pond or a small fish—they gain self-awareness. They begin to notice who they are in relation to others and how they can help others shine, or hinder them. They learn to recognize areas where they need to grow and develop. Through sports, children can begin to feel comfortable in their own skin.

When my (Margot's) daughter, Zoe, played basketball her sophomore year of high school, she didn't have as much experience as many of the girls on the team. She worked hard and in a number of games was in the starting five.

What I loved more than seeing my daughter run through a line of other players as her name was announced in the starting lineup, however, is what I saw of Zoe when she was on the bench. During time-outs and halftime pep talks, the athletes who'd been giving their all on the court were winded, sweaty, and thirsty. Zoe recognized this and developed the habit of filling cups of water for the players coming off the court. She hustled and she served with a smile.

When a child is benched, or when she's the star of the team, she has the opportunity to develop self-awareness. Either way, she can discover who she is in relation to others.

Socialization

Sports also have the potential to develop socialization in children. Something great happens when children learn how to play with other children. It happens in backyards and on playgrounds, and it can also happen in organized sports. Kids benefit from the opportunity to relate to a variety of personalities as they develop their own. They also have a unique opportunity to discover how to be themselves within the construct of a group. Sports can connect them with a diverse spectrum of people.

We also applaud the development of a type of league known as "Buddy Ball," in which children with physical and mental challenges are paired with peers who help them play ball. At the same time, the kids with special needs often end up instructing their able-bodied "buddies" in valuable lessons of sports and life, such as how to have fun, deal with hardship, contribute to a team, and prioritize friendship over winning and losing.

Sports provide rich opportunities for kids and families to embrace relationship with others.

Commitment

Third, sports are an opportunity for children to learn about commitment. In sports, children learn that practicing is how they'll improve. They discover what it takes to reach a goal. They discover not only what they have to do to become better players themselves but also what they need to do to help the team reach its goal. Sports can develop the deep value of commitment as children learn to sacrifice self for others.

We hear a lot of families tell their children who want to quit a sport, "If you started it, you finish it!" Even if we may be reluctant to admit it, our insistence is often driven by the fact that we paid for it! (Case in point: we don't get that hot under the collar when our teen's commitment to French Club begins to wane.) But sports really do provide an opportunity to develop commitment, particularly as you help your child understand what it means to be committed to a team and not just himself or herself. You help your child begin to ask, "What does it take for us to reach our goal?" And while she doesn't have control over anyone but herself, she can ask, "What do I have to do to be the best I can be to help our team reach its goal?"

My (Margot's) son Rollie has a friend named Omar, who was captain of the middle school soccer team. After Omar injured his foot one day during lunch hour, the team was without one of its most-skilled players for the last three games of the season. But Omar was cheering the team on from the bench, wearing a boot brace on his foot.

I expected that kind of participation and support from Omar, who is a wonderful young man. But I was more surprised to see Omar's family continuing to show up for games! His brother, dad, and grandfather remained loyal to the team even when they knew that Omar would never make it off the bench. This commitment signaled a great show of support for the team. But in a more subtle way, it also communicated to Omar that their relationship with him is not performance based. It allowed him to see that his family's commitment is to something larger than Omar.

Character

Finally, you can help your child understand that sports are an opportunity to be intentional about developing his or her character. On the field, on the court, in the gym, on the ice—there are countless opportunities for your child to make small decisions that will build or diminish his or her character. Too often we forget, or maybe never even realize, that that's why we play the games. It really isn't about the score, satisfying adult egos, determining which town is "better," or impressing any college coaches who come to watch. The reason we play is to provide everyone—players, coaches, and spectators—with opportunities to learn about themselves, others, and God.

Imagine that your daughter Courtney is playing soccer and finds herself with the ball in a breakaway situation. It's just her and the goalie, with her teammate Maria on her left. She knows what the coach has always said to do in this type of a two-on-one situation: "Keep the ball until the goalkeeper comes toward you, then pass it to your teammate for the easy score." While Courtney understands that, she has never scored a goal. And besides, Maria is always bragging about herself. So Courtney is facing a real dilemma.

All of these thoughts likely go through kids' minds in these situations. What a great opportunity you as a parent have, after

---

For people of faith: Three reasons to play

For kids who enjoy sports and are gifted athletically, we believe that it is the exact place where God wants to meet them. It is where they will learn the most about themselves, about others, and about God. But too often we see kids who've pushed, or been pushed, for years, and who suddenly wonder, "Why have I done this?"

Three questions can offer your child a new way to look at losing, playing with a ball hog, relating to coaches, befriending other players, and more. If you help your child who loves sports to consider these questions over the years, you'll help her understand that sports are an opportunity for personal and even spiritual growth.

1. What am I learning about myself?

2. What am I learning about others?

3. What am I learning about God?

Tip: Sports allow kids to learn about themselves, others, and God.

the game, to help Courtney process this and learn a lot about herself. Depending how you help your child navigate and understand his or her experience, sports have the potential to help shape your child. Athletics also provide an opportunity for parents to reflect for their children what characteristics they are recognizing in a child. When my (Margot's) son Abhi was playing soccer at seven years old, bravely weaving through boys twice his size, a mom next to me marveled, "He's fearless!" The word resonated deeply with what I knew to be true of my son. Six years later, another mom on the bench used the exact same word while watching Abhi play! These were opportunities for me to communicate to my son, "This is one of the neat qualities I see in you, and here are some others I've seen you display on the field." I shared with Abhi the ways I saw him being his very best self when playing soccer.

OPPORTUNITIES FOR ADULTS TO LIVE OUT THEIR VALUES

Whether we're athletes who've just gotten a bad call, the coach who helps the player recover from it, or fans in the stands tempted to yell at the ref because we care about the player who just got the bad call, sports give all of us this unique opportunity to live out the values we claim to possess.

Randy and Scott, friends from church who were raising boys who were both nine, coached their sons' Little League team together. Halfway through the season, a player named Jordan didn't show up for practice. When Randy and Scott learned that Jordan's mom's car had broken down, and that she was unable to get him to practices or games, they made a commitment to transport Jordan for the rest of the season.

One church in central Pennsylvania hosts a "community cleat bank," to which families can bring used cleats and can look for shoes in the size that their child needs. Families save money and help out other families, especially those in need who can't afford to drop a load of cash at Dick's Sporting Goods. People are joining in this recycling effort through the support of a local congregation. And the greatest thing? You don't need to donate a pair to take a pair. No one keeps score.

Besides the hands-on opportunities for service, shepherding players or offering cleats, there are more macro issues in sports into which Christians can speak.

One troubling reality I (Dave) have recognized during my professional career is the way in which men's sports are prioritized over women's sports. For example, men's sports are almost always on the front page of the sports section of newspapers and women's sports are inside, often buried between other stories. Though I can't change the entire culture of sports in this regard, I do want to call us to accountability when it comes to equal support for men's and women's, boys' and girls', sports.

After I began my job at a Christian university, I was surprised to find that a community that espouses high standards for justice and equality demonstrated an imbalance in its support of athletes at men's and women's games. While I admit that some people may find players who are bigger, faster, and stronger more exciting to watch, every game holds the inherent opportunity to learn lessons about life.

Halfway through one of my first basketball seasons, I noticed the evident discrepancy between the number of fans coming out for men's basketball games and those showing up to support our women. The imbalance disturbed me to the point of drafting an email to the campus community. It was one of those moments when I may have hit "send" too quickly:

It's obvious that this community prefers to watch men's sports more than women's sports. I acknowledge that men's games can be more exciting and, to some of you, more enjoyable. But I'm concerned about the message this sends to our female athletes. And I'm concerned about what it says about you and our community. Please remember that these sporting events are not about you; they are about the men and women, and they deserve our support. Please give me a reason to set up the extra bleachers for a women's game. Let's not succumb to the current culture norm that values men more than women.

Warmly,
Dave King

Thankfully, I kept my job.

When athletes come to our program at Eastern Mennonite University, they won't find Scripture verses painted on gym walls or locker-room mirrors. They won't hear public prayers before a game. They most likely won't see the teams pray together after a game or have devotions before practices or games. It's not that these activities aren't valued, but we don't require them.

What they *will* find are Christian coaches who are living out their faith daily and modeling what it means to be disciples of Christ in the world of college sports. These coaches accept everyone regardless of their faith tradition or where they are in their faith journey. They purpose to be people who are "planting seeds" in the lives of students, realizing that they may not see the results. Young people who enter college with the sole purpose of playing a sport are exposed to an alternative lifestyle that values sports but places a greater value on the whole person and that person's faith and vocation. I'd suggest that every coach at every level has that opportunity to live out their convictions as significant people in players' lives.

If you're holding this book, there's a likelihood that at some point you or a family member has been a volunteer or paid coach. I count coaching a privilege and an opportunity to grow personally and to invest in children's lives.

Investing in children not our own

One of my (Margot's) friends, Chris Lahr, is a general manager for Timoteo, a football league in the Kensington neighborhood of Philadelphia. Through Timoteo, Chris and other Christian men are reaching out in love to the male youth of the Kensington community. In partnership with local churches and organizations, Timoteo empowers these caring adults to mentor youth through athletics. These mentors spend time with kids and offer spiritual formation while doing something that the kids love to do: play football.

Chris describes what he sees in these young people: "We see kids come to us who can't catch a football. Before long they're catching the football and they're actually becoming good at it. Not long after that, they see they can excel in other areas of their lives as well." The confidence being developed in these teens ripples out well beyond athletics. Chris raves, "We now have kids going to college who never thought it was a possibility. They're the first in their families to go."

One father, while speaking with Chris, pointed toward his son on the field and said that, among all his children, this boy was "the worst one." But the father went on to say that he could see the impact Timoteo was making both in his son's life and in the wider community. Chris affirms, "Because of Timoteo, this young man's life has changed. He finished school and is stepping up as a leader in the community."

Through Timoteo and mentors like Chris, young men are glimpsing the gracious face of a God who smiles upon them and equips them to become all that they were created to be. This ministry shines as one of the brightest examples of the potential we see sports can have in young lives: forming young people into who they were created to be.

Christlikeness

For Christian families, we believe athletics are a unique opportunity to explore and demonstrate foundational and formational values like service and sacrifice. And because we believe that God is with us at all times, we also affirm that every one of our experiences—including successes and failures in sports—can help shape our Christlikeness.

There are a handful of popular Scriptures that Christian sports ministries emblazon on T-shirts, and one of our favorites—a passage that we believe has real meat to it—is 2 Peter 1:3-9. Peter begins by saying that we have everything we need for life and godliness through our knowledge of Christ. Then he

Dinnertime conversation starters

Use these scenarios to start conversations with your kids. In each case, discuss what the scenario might look like for your child's sport. Recall a real-life situation when this happened to your child, a friend, a teammate, or an opponent. For each question ask, "How have you responded? How might you respond?"

1. **Erroneous decision from an official**
   The official in charge of your athletic competition makes a bad call or decision.

2. **Teammate who cheats**
   You notice a teammate cheating in a competition.

3. **Coach behaving badly**
   One of your coaches is behaving badly.

4. **Parent behaving badly**
   You are worried that the parent of one of your teammates is behaving in a harmful manner toward your teammate.

5. **Competing for position**
   You and one other athlete are competing for the same opportunity.

goes on to list Christlike qualities, or attributes, that we should have: faith, goodness, knowledge, self-control, endurance, godliness, mutual affection, and love for others.

Of these Peter asserts, "For if you possess these qualities in increasing measure, they will keep you from being ineffective and unproductive in your knowledge of our Lord Jesus Christ" (2 Peter 1:8).

All athletes know what happens to them if they don't improve their skills: they become ineffective and unproductive and sit on the bench! So we should always be asking our children and ourselves: Have we used our sports experiences to achieve those growth goals? Are we more patient, gracious, kind, and loving than we were a few seasons ago?

We serve our children well as we help shift their thinking about sports (and ours!) from personal *gain*—getting "unbenched," winning, being voted captain, earning a scholarship—to personal *growth*. We do that as we reflect on the ways we've seen growth and also, much more gently, the opportunities we recognize in which there's room to be transformed more and more into the image of Christ.

LASTING VALUES

One of my (Dave's) greatest joys as an athletics director is running into an alumnus ten years down the road who says, "I remember this particular experience, and it's addressing what I'm facing right now." It reminds me why I do what I do.

A few years ago I was invited to present a workshop at a denominational youth convention. We were doing an exercise to help youth consider what they were learning from sports at the time and how it might translate into their lives in the future. So I offered them a few scenarios that I'd witnessed in game situations. Then I asked them to consider what emotions and attitudes contributed to that situation, and what they imagine might happen in ten or twelve years that the situation might relate to.

The final scenario I offered was a basketball team in the state tournament. Team A has outplayed its opponent throughout the entire game. With two seconds left in the game, the official makes a questionable traveling call against a player on Team A. The ref gives the ball back to Team B, whose player throws the ball inbounds to a teammate who pivots and swishes a basket from half-court. Team B wins the state championship.

Brutal, right? If you've been in that situation, you know the pain, the knot in the pit of your stomach that just hurts. You've felt that deep ache that just lingers. You've known the loss, anger, and frustration that life just isn't *fair*.

"Okay," I opened with the youth, "let's talk about what the feelings were."

The teens engaged immediately.

One offered, "I'd be angry at the official."

"It kind of comes down to luck of the draw at that point, right?" another chimed in.

"If I was the person who'd traveled, it would feel rough."

"So," I pressed, "can anybody think of a situation down the road in life where this might help? Where going through this experience might inform a future one?"

"Not getting hired for a job."

"Losing the bid on a construction job to your competitor."

"Someone running a stop sign and totaling your new car."

Then a young man in the front row quietly offered one word.

"Miscarriage," he said.

I'm not usually speechless, but in that moment I was.

Somewhere in that young man's life he'd known someone who'd endured the miscarriage of a child. In some way he understood that a loss in a game situation—that pain, the sick feeling in the pit of his stomach—might help others when they experience a more profound loss, failure, or unfairness down the road.

Ideally, our young athletes will carry lessons like this into their future lives—lessons that will form them into more self-aware, compassionate, and committed followers of Christ. Along with questionable values that we can help our children to identify and reject, sports provide opportunities for young people and their families to implement the values they *do* hold.

Q&A with Margot

Question: How do I know what values youth sports are teaching my kid? When he plays a sport, he's outside. Isn't that enough?

Answer: Have you been reading my diary? I count any minute that my children are outdoors, unplugged, as a win. So I get it.

But I do think it's worth noticing the values that are being communicated to our children even when they're never clearly articulated: "Play through the pain." "Winners are more valuable than losers." "Competitions are more important than family." Our children are *really* savvy and swallow these naughty lies whole. When you notice these myths, expose them by discussing them with your kids.

And I also encourage you to identify the values you do hold dear and to help your kids find tangible ways to live them out.

- Compassion: "When another player is hurt, from your team or the other team, you be the first one there to comfort and help."

- Generosity: "Let's cut up a cold watermelon together to share with other kids at practice."

- Self-control: "When players are gossiping, either keep your mouth shut or shut the gossip down."

- Kindness: "At every practice or game, try to speak with a kid on the team with a physical or intellectual difference."

- Humility: "Accept responsibility for errors rather than blaming team members."

You get the idea. As you let your children know what you value—and as you live out those same values!—you bless your kids and help them become who God made them to be.

Myth Six

Good Parents Attend All Their Children's Games

Not many people can say that they have hired themselves. Fewer can say that they then promptly fired themselves.

During the time I worked as athletics director at a Christian high school, I (Dave) hired myself to coach ninth-grade boys' basketball. Following our 0–19 season, I fired myself from the same coaching job.

I'm not sure, but that might be some kind of a record—one I'm not proud of. (Hey, we were desperate.)

As the season concluded, we decided to put our nineteen defeats behind us by wrapping up with a pizza party. I wanted to process the experience of a losing season with the guys, so I asked them how the experience had been for them and what we might have done differently.

Between bites of pizza they offered, "We could have spent more time practicing our shooting," "We really needed a tall player," and one even queried, "Are there other teams we could have played?"

But then one young man said, "You know, Mr. King, if you would have taken away the scoreboard and the parents, I would have done a whole lot better."

I laughed, but the comment stuck with me. I think it actually struck something deep inside me that I'd noticed but not clearly articulated.

This player's innocent comment is actually what started me on this journey to understand where the youth sports train jumped the track. It was the first red flag that told me something wasn't quite right in youth sports today.

In the last several decades, we have witnessed parents' behavior—toward refs, toward coaches, and even toward their own child athletes—becoming increasingly troubling. And we don't mean only the lunatic parents who assault referees. We mean typical parents like the ones in your neighborhood, book club, or church. We mean parents who truly want "what's best" for their children—but who have been fed a lie about what that means.

One of those lies is that "good parents" attend every game. Its wily logic has convinced us:

If you really love your child, you'll leave work early and race across town to show up for the last twelve minutes of his game.

If you really value family, then you'll coerce all her siblings to sit in the bleachers at every game.

If you were a better parent, you'd take even more time off work to travel to the away games like the parents who are really committed to their children do.

But what if we could convince you that, for most children, parent attendance at competitions means much more to the parent than it does to the child? What would be different for you if we could persuade you that children actually need and deserve a space where they can just play with other kids? Or what would you say if we told you that your child actually performed better when he didn't have the pressure—spoken or unspoken—of "performing" for his parents and grandparents?

What we'd love you to hear and believe is this: being the best parent you can be—the one your child needs—might be a lot easier than what you've got going right now.

PARENTS ARE NUTTY

If you're familiar with sports, you know that in high school and college, preseason scrimmages are often held so that players can get a feel for playing together, coaches can try out different plays and combinations of players, and the team has an opportunity for a "dry run." Most league rules specify not only that scores not be kept at these games but also that the games not even be announced to the public.

So you can imagine my (Dave's) surprise when, working in my office at Lancaster Mennonite High School one year, I received a phone call requesting I come and pull out the stacking bleachers for the basketball scrimmage.

"Pull the bleachers out?" I asked the assistant coach who'd dialed my office. "Why would we do that?"

"Well," he said sheepishly, "there are about one hundred parents over here."

"Really?" I asked. "You have got to be kidding me."

Though I don't think smoke was really coming out of my ears, it felt like it might be. I pulled myself together as I made my way to the gym. I thought seriously about not even going, since they should have known the rules and I wasn't going to appease them.

Standing in front of the crowd of parents, representing players from both teams, I calmly let them know, "I'm not going to pull the bleachers out. Scrimmages are not public events, so we've made no arrangements for providing seating in the bleachers. I suppose if you want to be here you can sit on the floor."

So they sat on the floor, although quite a few found folding chairs in classrooms and brought them into the gym. But I do know that many of them kept score (the scoreboard wasn't on), and they could even tell you how many points each player had.

Driving home that evening and reflecting on the events of the day, I realized that this event had been another red flag for me—a signal that something is not quite right in youth sports culture.

As an educator, I've always been baffled by parents who can find a way to make it to twenty basketball games in a season but who can't attend the one parent-teacher meeting held every year! The sports pull is strong. I get that. High expectations for athletes and parents seem to have become the norm. And as parents, we often accept those norms—conforming to the pattern of the world—without much thought.

Our friend Mark enjoyed telling us about one of his football practices. As he gathered the team of eleven- and twelve-year-olds together, he noticed about four or five parents sitting at the edge of the field. He didn't quite understand their presence, given that this was just a practice. About halfway through practice, he took the team to the other end of the field to work with the blocking dummies. As the drill started, he noticed that the parents had picked up their lawn chairs and made their way to the other end of the field. Immediately after the drill, he took the team back to the other end where practice had started. And sure enough: the parents and their lawn chairs returned.

At the next practice, Mark informed his assistant coach that he was going to be doing something a bit different today and he advised him to keep his eye on the parents. So Mark started practice on one end, took the team to the other end for the drills with the dummies, then took them to another section of the field. He continued this pattern for each different segment of practice. Finally, one parent yelled out to Mark, "What are you doing—trying to get us in shape?" Those parents were so focused on their sons' performance that they missed a great opportunity to simply sit and visit with each other.

Over the last several decades, the involvement of parents and grandparents in youth sports has reached epic proportions. While parents complain about being so busy, many of them are still at every game their child plays, and most of the practices. These parents have heard the message from somewhere, loud and clear, that being a good parent requires attending every single one of your child's athletic events.

We are aware that while some parents are harried by these efforts, a lot of us genuinely enjoy watching our children and their friends engage in athletic competition. We delight in our kids the way that God delights in us. We understand that maternal and paternal impulse.

But we'd still love to encourage moderation. We can support our children and be involved in their lives without being omnipresent. Take your spouse out for coffee. Go do the grocery shopping. During one or two games a month, do *anything* else. Do not be controlled or ruled by your child's schedule. You need time for you. (Don't wait for children to take the lead on this one; they won't have any way to appreciate the breather it provides for them until they experience it!)

Our concern really isn't that parents aren't getting enough caffeine. Our concern is what is being communicated by parents' constant presence. Even when we mean well, there's a high likelihood that what we will communicate to our children is that we value them based on their *performance*. Do we crouch over their shoulder and cheer them on when they're reading a book? Do we shout encouragement when they're eating tacos? Do we hover near the fence of a backyard birthday party after we drop our child off? Though we may never verbalize it, the implicit message children can receive is this: *My parent is there for me only if I'm performing.*

Sometimes we notice some parents who show up to every game at the beginning of a season. But when their child doesn't see a lot of playing time, these parents stop showing up at the game. Without ever meaning to, what they've communicated to that child is *I'll be there for you only when you're performing.*

We can do better.

We realize that many parents are performing a daily juggling act that includes managing the needs of children, spouses, employers, pets, and sometimes parents or in-laws. Even the best jugglers, though, still need to meet their own needs if they're going to be nourished to care for others. It's a bit like applying your own oxygen mask before helping others on the aircraft. Jesus' admonition to love others the way we love ourselves is predicated on the assumption that we are loving ourselves. And though other stressed, harried parents might communicate, even unwittingly, that we shouldn't take time for ourselves—to be refreshed physically, emotionally, socially, and spiritually—it's actually the way we're fueled to love others well.

GOOD PARENTS ARE . . .

So how true is it that parents' omnipresence *benefits* children?

The two of us had different experiences of our parents' involvement in youth sports. Interestingly enough, however, our two rather opposite experiences cause each of us to question this myth.

My (Dave's) dad didn't come to any of my games when I was growing up. While I'd be on the court or the diamond or the field, he'd be at home mowing the lawn or working around the house. Knowing my dad, a no-nonsense guy living in the middle part of the twentieth century, I suspect he would have even considered sitting at a child's sporting competition to be a waste of time. I'm sincere when I report that it didn't bother me. Honestly, my dad's absence made that space and time mine. It was a gift he gave me. And when I did get home after a game, we didn't spend a lot of time talking about it. I just gave him a quick recap, and then we went on to something else. And when he did take a break from working, we'd play ball together in the backyard. Simply put, my dad just didn't consider sitting in the stands necessary. The most cherished times with my dad were when we played together on the church softball team. He was the pitcher and I was the catcher. Those were special times! And I think I turned out okay.

On the other hand, my (Margot's) mom reports that she attended all my games. Interestingly enough, I don't remember my mother's presence at a single one! When I suited up, my attention was on the ball, my teammates, my coach, and my opponents. I really didn't have much energy left to be noticing who was in the stands! I certainly felt my mom's support in the ways she made a lot of athletic opportunities possible—registering for leagues, buying the gear I needed, driving to games, washing my uniforms—but her presence in the bleachers wasn't really on my radar. I'll let other people be the judge of this, but I think I turned out okay.

This limited, not-very-scientific sample suggests to us that parents value the idea of being omnipresent to children more than children do!

Some children, like the high school student we mentioned at the beginning of the chapter who would have loved to play in a parent-free gym, are keenly aware of their parents' presence. But ideally, children, who are naturally egocentric, aren't thinking about their parents while they are playing sports. Ideally, they're thinking about the game. They're reviewing a new play in their minds. They're focusing one hundred percent of their attention on the next pitch. They're looking for a teammate on the field hockey field to whom they can pass. Typically, naturally, they're not thinking about the spectators. And if a parent has made herself so noticeable in the bleachers that a child's attention is focused on his parent, tuned in to the parent's voice or gesture or excessive emotion—well, suffice to say, that that's not necessarily in the child's best interest!

And even though it's pretty natural for a child to not think too much about our presence, we've inflated the idea of "good parents are always there" to superhuman proportions.

I (Margot) recall reading a book by the CEO of an international ministry that served the poor. In his biography, I discovered that, admirably, this man, a father of two, wanted his family to be a priority in the midst of his busy life of international travel. Yet what I remember—*all* I remember—from the book was a statement this Christian leader made: throughout his daughters' high school athletic careers, he'd never missed one of their games.

That single fact stuck in my craw like the irritating shell of a popcorn kernel.

Never missed a game?! I reasoned to myself, almost to the point of madness. I miss a game every week! I have three children playing soccer every Saturday in the spring between the hours of nine in the morning and noon, often on three different fields in my city. It is not physically possible for me—a stay-at-home mom who's not the CEO of an international organization—to go one or two weeks without missing one of my children's games.

And though logic told me that my "goodness" as a mom didn't depend on my perfect attendance, and common sense told me that this guy's story couldn't possibly be true, a naughty little voice hissed that I might not be as good of a mom as I should be.

On our best days, we can reassure ourselves that we're a little bit better than the dad who's never made it to one game and a lot better than the crazy parent who gets kicked out of peewee lacrosse for verbally attacking the ref. But on our bad days, burdened by the myth that our constant presence is what makes us good parents, we suspect that we're not measuring up.

What we want every parent to know is that your kid will be okay. In fact, because it is quite typical for a child to believe that her relationship with the parent who's deeply invested in watching her perform is performance based—a valid assumption, we think!—it might even benefit your relationship to step away a bit.

We know: it's mind-boggling. But sit with it a bit and let it soak in.

THE SURPRISING TRUTH

Because we both believe that most parents have the very best of intentions, we want to expose the faulty logic that drives some of us to attempt superhuman feats of omnipresence and suffocates us with guilt when we don't measure up.

Being constantly present to our children—at practices, scrimmages, in-season games, off-season games, postseason games—is predicated on the faulty assumption that our presence is what's best for them. (Admittedly, it's easy to believe.)

But that's simply not been proven to be the case!

According to a recent study, parents who overvalue their children—which is revealed in parents' beliefs that their child is more special than others or more deserving—contribute to increased rates of narcissism in children. Children who are made to believe that the world does, and should, revolve around them are destined for difficult relationships in adulthood.

And while they no doubt believe that they're engaging out of love for their children, parents who are hyper-involved in their kids' lives might actually not be spurred by love at all.

In a previous chapter, we mentioned extrinsic and intrinsic values and how they might apply to youth sports. Constant parental presence at sporting events can be an extrinsic motivator, similar to the big trophies, newspaper articles, new uniforms, and hotel stays. And if you recall, the introduction of extrinsic values too early in life inhibits the development of intrinsic values. And it is intrinsic motivators that keep a person engaged, committed, and in love with a sport.

One of the difficult transitions from high school to collegiate sports is getting used to long bus or van trips to places you don't know and then playing in front of twenty-five people. Whether or not your high school team was good, there were usually a lot of people at the game: parents, friends, teachers, and maybe church friends. Many times the games were a community event. At the collegiate level, those deep connections aren't always there, and parents are often hours away from the college. So if players have relied on parents and fans to give their sports experience meaning, they may have a difficult time adjusting to college.

THE RISKS

Though we might be tempted to identify a parent's commitment to her child's athletic life as "loving" or "sacrificial," there are risks to parents' overinvolvement in their children's athletic lives.

When parents attend every game, the chance of developing a parent-child relationship that is based on performance increases

While this may never be your intention, you may be inadvertently communicating to your child that you will only be present to her when she is performing. In addition, you have opened up the possibility that your child will link her value and self-worth to her success as an athlete. In his book, *Will You Still Love Me If I Don't Win?*, Christopher Andersonn points out,

> Young children are young, impressionable and prone to making snap judgments about themselves. As parents we are responsible to help them learn that they do not have to do or be something to be loved. They are lovable and worthwhile just as they are. And that worthwhile part of them can never be lost. It is not something they can earn or lose. It is God-given and it is with them every moment of their lives.

Tip: Dial back your involvement when your child is performing, and amp it up when she's not.

When parents attend every game, a child's development of responsibility can be impeded

When parents are overly involved—seeking out competitive club teams online, printing and managing registration forms for older kids, laundering their older child's stinky gear every night and presenting it folded and ready to go the next day—children can fail to develop responsibility.

During my (Dave's) ten years at the collegiate level, I have seen a dramatic increase in many young athletes' sense of entitlement. While I am no longer surprised when this happens, I am always frustrated when I, or one of our coaches, receive calls from parents about a situation with their son's or daughter's team. I have started to take the position that unless or until the college student comes to me to discuss the issue, I will not respond to the parent other than to let him know that I will address it with the player. It is very tough for parents to learn to let go and allow the child to handle some matters. But it is necessary if young people are going to develop into healthy adults who have tools to deal with what life gives them.

Tip: If your child is able to do it for himself, let him do it himself.

When parents attend every game, the sport can become more important to the parent than to the child

When you put more into the sport than your child, you may fail to see that it has ceased to be life-giving for your child. Recognizing that the sport means more to a parent than it does to a child is tough for parents. It is why we overanalyze the game in the van on the way home. Frankly, the most important event of the day for your child might not have been the game at all but a disturbing conversation he had at school—or maybe even the new eraser he got from his teacher. Are you ready to listen to your child talk about things other than sports? The game is, and always will be (or should be), the child's event. Let him enjoy it.

As the sport becomes more important to the parent (or grandparent) than it is to the child, the likelihood of irrational behavior increases. A child psychologist in Indiana told us that while most of us believe "we could never do that" when we hear about a parent physically attacking a coach, player, or official, the reality is that we are all capable of such actions. Having someone take away from us something that we hold of high value—our child's sports success, in this case—could easily trigger irrational behavior.

Tip: Let your child steer the ship. Provide young kids opportunities to sample different sports, but let older children beg you to increase their involvement!

When parents attend every game, communication decreases because everyone saw the game

One of the great benefits of athletics to children and adolescents comes when they have the opportunity to reflect on their own experience. If everyone in the family saw the game, and siblings and parents crowd the minivan with their own opinions, athletes lose the opportunity to let parents know what they got out of it. It actually robs them of the opportunity to process the events of the day and learn to articulate them to others. You may not get the information you want when you skip a game and let your child tell you about it, but you will get a fresh perspective.

Tip: Skip a game or create intentional space in the wake of a competition for your athlete to reflect.

When parents attend every game, children lose private space away from parents

As children grow and develop, they benefit in the context of safe spaces where they have increasing autonomy from parents. We're not saying that you shouldn't be present at all. We're not saying that you shouldn't get as much background as you can on the coach, the league, and some of the other families. But while we as parents might be a bit fearful of our child spending a lot of time with families who have different values, the alternative—having you watch their every action and reaction—won't help your child learn to process the situation.

Tip: Let practices, and a number of games, be times in which you let your child spread her wings a bit.

When parents attend every game, it interferes with effectiveness of coaches

Parents' constant presence compromises a coach's influence and also creates a situation that isn't fair to your child. For years, your child's antennae have been tipped toward your face and voice, but a natural part of his development is to learn from other adult authorities. Give your child the gift of that opportunity.

Mike Matheny, manager of the St. Louis Cardinals, penned the most valuable piece of communication from coach to parent we have ever seen. It was addressed to the parents of the boys on the Little League team he was coaching in the years between his playing career and the start of his coaching at the professional level. Matheny's letter went viral, and has become known as The Matheny Manifesto. As for parental involvement, Matheny writes,

> The best situation for all of us is for you to plan on handing these kids over to me and the assistant coaches when you drop them off and plan on them being mine for the 2 or so hours that we have scheduled for a game or practice. I would like for these boys to have some responsibility for having their own water, not needing you to keep running to the concession stand or having parents behind the dugout asking their son if they are thirsty, or hungry, or too hot and please share this information with other invited guests . . . like grandparents.

Tip: Be invisible at practices. During games, be the quietest parent in the bleachers.

When parents attend every game, family time is redefined because it becomes centered on the athlete

Children experience security when they know that the adults are the glue that holds the family together. A family that begins to revolve around an athlete, especially when there are other siblings, becomes lopsided.

While we love our children, they should not rule our lives. Yes, we need to give them unconditional love and the time they deserve, but we are also responsible to take care of ourselves. It's well known that during the child-rearing years, parents often focus their relationship on their children instead of each other. And in this season of life, when parents can't afford to forsake their relationship, practices and games actually offer built-in time to nurture it! Skipping a practice or even a game to have coffee, go shopping, or visit a museum with your spouse will likely be more beneficial to your entire family than getting tense on the sidelines.

Tip: Develop authentic practices of family time together that don't involve all but one family member watching the athlete.

When parents attend every game, they may miss subtle cues that their child is not enjoying the sport anymore

A lot of parents who are overly involved simply miss the signs that the game has become more about themselves than about their children. When kids are pushed by parents, rather than playing because they like playing the game, they'll burn out and quit.

One of the faces of burnout is a mysterious "injury." One of the challenges for athletic trainers is to determine who is really injured and who might be trying to avoid practice, call attention to themselves (since they aren't playing), or not face the reality that another player is better at his position. If a player is losing interest in the game or not playing as much, an "injury" helps her avoid the reality of the situation. Don't miss this subtle message.

Tip: Check in regularly with your child to get a fresh sense of whether he is still enjoying the game.

When parents attend every game, they can become overly involved

You've heard of helicopter parents, who hover over their children even to the detriment of children developing necessary life skills. A recent mutation of the helicopter parent is the lawn mower parent. If helicopter parents are supervising play practice, adding extra batting practice on the weekends, and completing an unfinished science fair diorama for a sixth grader, lawn mower parents are clearing the path in front of their children before they take a step. They're managing their student's group projects in the high school. They're contacting college admissions departments on behalf of their children. They're even calling employers when their grown children have job interviews!

Believe us: we get it. When my (Dave's) son was playing ball and the guy or gal in the striped shirt made a call, I'd often wonder how the ref could do that to my kid! How could the ref interfere with his success? And when my (Margot's) middle- and high-school-aged children would have a rough season with a particular coach—clearly the coach's fault, since my children are sinless angels—I was tempted to contact the school's athletics director to register my complaint. So we're familiar with the impulse.

Lawn mower parents, though, interfere in their children's experience before they even have it! They'll reveal, in conversation with their child's high school coach, that their child who plays goalie has much more elite experience than the student athlete who might be her competition. They'll make sure a coach is aware of the prestigious camp across the country their child attended over the summer. They'll offer to access any extra private coaching that might give their child an extra edge.

At the college level, it's not uncommon for these parents to call the athletics director about the amount of playing time their children receive. After their grown child's job interview at a local business, lawn mower parents may call an employer on their child's behalf! They don't want anything to slow down their child, and they'll clear a path in front of her if they think it will help.

Tip: As soon as she is able, let your child be in charge of her sporting experience.

When parents attend every game, they sometimes behave badly

The parents doing the lawn-chair shuffle, moving their chairs up and down the field to monitor that football practice, are a fairly benign intrusion compared to some. We've probably all seen one or two parents who go too far, yelling at their kids, the team-mates, the officials, or the coach. But there are a multitude of ways parents can interfere with their child's experience of sports.

A few years ago I (Dave) noticed that at halftime of a soccer game, when the coach was talking to the team, a dad on the periphery of the team circle was giving his son advice while his son needed to be listening to the coach. Finally, the coach stopped his teaching and said to the kid, "Are you here?" I didn't know the parent. Maybe he was an alumnus of Major League Soccer or even an Olympic coach. Maybe. Regardless, he compromised his son's experience by imposing his own agenda.

"Phew," you may sigh, "at least I'm not as bad as *that* parent."

The two of us consider ourselves students of human nature, and we notice that one of the ways we let ourselves off the hook is by reassuring ourselves that we're not nearly as nutty as the next parent is. "Clearly Heidi's parents are the ones with real problems," we may tell ourselves. "We're not half that bad!" And we may not be. But simply because we can point a finger at a parent who's more out of control than we think we are doesn't mean that we're serving the best interest of the child who's been entrusted to us.

The goal is never to be "less awful" than another parent. It's not to be a "little bit better" than another adult who's completely deranged. Those are both defense mechanisms that allow us to continue to behave badly, to the detriment of our children.

Tip: Check your impulse to compare yourself to other, *more horrible*, parents.

The real job—every parent's growing edge—is to consider what's best for our children, and be willing to adjust our own behavior to benefit our kids and our communities.

When I (Margot) discussed this phenomenon of overly involved parents with my daughter, Zoe, really looking for a free pass to get some errands done during game time, Zoe let me know that she does value her parents' presence at her games. So I have now factored that in to our attendance.

But I also feel the judgment of other parents because I don't attend every game.

As Zoe, who typically plays goalkeeper, ran out onto the field to play forward for the first time, a parent in the bleachers innocently remarked to me, "Did you come because you knew she'd play?"

"Nope," I replied, feeling the burning sting of shame, but also confident in my choice. "Just a coincidence!"

Ouch.

Though it wasn't a Hallmark feel-good parenting moment, which a lot of our choices won't be, it was a moment when I could affirm that, by balancing the needs of my whole family, I actually had been doing what I've been called to do. That's the admittedly unwieldy math of Christian parents: we're called to live out our values as we honor both the family members who share a roof with us and the neighbors God loves who don't.

IDEAS FOR CHANGE

If you want to be free of the wily myth insisting that "good parents attend every game," we challenge you to miss at least two games. Just skip them. Mark it on your calendar when the schedule comes out. Let your child know, "I'm not coming to these games, and it's not because I have a meeting at church or have to work late. It's because I want you to experience it yourself."

After that game, ask your child about the game when she gets home. Guess what? She probably isn't going to tell you what you want to hear, because she won't be analyzing the game. She might say "It was good" or "We lost by fifty points." We don't know what she'll say! But we do know that she'll have had the opportunity to process it herself and explain it to you in her terms, children's terms. And that will be a great gift that you have given to her, even if you don't get the information about the game that you were looking for.

When we have shared this suggestion with audiences in churches and other organizations, invariably a relieved parent or grandparent pulls us aside to thank us for giving them permission to miss a game! So hear us clearly: permission granted.

Again: we're not giving you permission to be a slacker parent. In fact, we may be giving you permission to be a *better* parent. (Watch with amazement as you share this really good news with your peers in the bleachers! Come Saturday, you could become somebody's hero.)

Five ways to ruin your child's sports experience

1. Analyze the results of the game. Begin by asking, "What was the score?"

2. Analyze your child's performance. Begin by asking, "How many points/goals/runs did you score?"

3. Analyze the team's performance. Begin by asking, "Why did she do that? What was wrong with her today?"

4. Analyze the coach's performance. Begin by asking, "What was he thinking?!"

5. Analyze the referee's performance. Begin by asking, "Was she blind?!"

Tip: An excellent alternative to dissecting the team or your player is to seek out your child's experience of the game or practice.

Better yet, when you drop off your child at practice or a game, scoop up one of the other parents and share some coffee or a run to the grocery store. Chances are you will return to the field after practice or after the game as parents with more resources. And we don't just mean caffeine or groceries. We mean that you've been nourished by friendship, which is a win for your kids.

A PARENT WHO GETS IT

When Elliot had a few great plays in one inning as catcher for the Durham School of the Arts Bulldogs, I (Margot) couldn't help myself from sneaking up to the dugout and letting him know that he'd been a big help to the team. Elliot's mom wasn't at the game yet, so I kept my eye open for her arrival so that I could brag about Elliot's great game.

I noticed Elliot's sister slide into the bleachers, but I couldn't find his mom. His sister sidled up to the fence to film him with her phone when he batted. Still no mom. Because the game was at a pretty remote field in town, I wondered how Elliot's sister had made it there without parental assistance.

Finally, near the end of the game, I saw Elliot's mom, Jaylynn, slowly creeping toward the field from the parking lot.

I rushed over to let Jaylynn know that her boy had had a particularly amazing third inning, throwing out two players who tried, unsuccessfully, to steal home.

As we chatted, Jaylynn shared with me that her children, both athletes, had banned her from being one of those loud cheering parents in the bleachers. Although everyone else might be cheering, they'd explained to her, they could pick out her voice in a crowd and it sort of rattled them. They felt like they could perform better if she wasn't around. Or at least if she was silent.

Because the team bus wouldn't be taking kids back to school, parents had to show up at the game to gather their young. And when Jaylynn did, she would typically hover in the wooded area behind the dugout or linger in the bushes near the parking lot. She was a mom who loved her kiddos and wanted to honor their wishes to let the game be their own.

As we continued to chat, I discovered that Jaylynn is a bit of an expert on parenting and has a doctorate in psychology.

Of course she does. By listening carefully to her kids and being secure enough in her relationship with them, she knew they would know they were loved even if she didn't follow the "good parent" rule of youth sports culture.

The ones brave enough to linger in the woods or walk around the track with a friend often are.

Q&A with Dave

Question: Dave, I cheer from the bleachers to support and encourage my child or grandchild. What's so wrong with that?

Answer: I understand the impulse of parents and grandparents to be there to support a child. I do. I enjoyed watching all three of my kids play. And I'm a new grandparent, with two wonderful granddaughters. I get it. I enjoy watching the video clips of them in the Christmas play at church or Hula-Hooping in the backyard. And in a few years, if my granddaughters get involved in youth sports, you may run into me in the bleachers when I visit my son's family

But here's one thing I can guarantee: at a kids' sports game, you are not going to hear me say anything.

I determined a long time ago that I would never say anything at my children's games. Maybe it began because, as an athletics director, I was responsible for crowd control and needed to be neutral and to maintain a calm presence. I also realized that there were plenty of others who would say something.

The main reason I've made this choice, though, is that shouting out encouragements, instructions, and cheers to kids who are competing can cause confusion about what the coach has instructed the player. It's possible what I'm yelling for her to do is completely contrary to what the coach told her to do!

Even encouraging words can create pressure to please with performance. I understand that to suggest remaining silent in the stands flies in the face of conventional practice. But if you listen to the words you're saying—"You can do this" and "You've got this one"—even the best words imply that you value success above all else. It's why some leagues are enforcing "Silent Saturdays," which are designated days when no one is allowed to talk—even the coach! The only ones allowed to speak or yell are the kids.

If you choose to extend encouragement to players, listen carefully to what you're saying and be intentional about the words you choose.

Margot told me about the dad of a child on her son's summer league baseball team. In the most critical moments of a game—when his son is pitching and the bases are loaded, or when he's got two strikes and a third ends the inning—this dad yells out two surprising words: "Have fun!" That this is the kid on the team who does have fun doing his best and enjoying the game comes as no surprise.

Find creative ways to let your young athlete know that, succeed or fail, you are *for* him or her.

Myth Seven

The Money We Are Investing into Youth Sports Will Pay Off

The Bergman family shared their story with me (Dave) when I first moved to Virginia.

Mark and Beth's son Aaron participated in a nine-year-old travel baseball league one summer, played in three tournaments, and had a great experience. But the Bergmans balked when, after signing him up for ten-year-old travel ball, they received the team's schedule. The ten-year-olds would play nine weekend tournaments during the summer. The Bergmans, who also had another son, Jared, added the cost of the travel and hotel rooms and calculated that the experience would cost more than $3,000. For one sport. One season. One child.

The Bergmans asked me what they should do. Was it worth investing this much money into their young son's athletic career? They didn't mention scholarships explicitly, but that was the implication.

"You're asking the wrong guy," I warned them.

I often say this to parents who ask me for advice about kids' elite leagues and travel teams. I sometimes think they expect a certain answer from me. Surely, as an athletics director at a university, I'll support their decision to help young athletes get better. Surely I'll agree with the coach of the elite team who wants their son or daughter to play.

Wrong.

Truth be told, when parents ask me for my opinion, I usually end up advising them to make a choice that few other families are making.

The Bergmans assured me that they really wanted my opinion. So I gave it to them.

"My biggest concern," I explained, "is that somewhere along the line, you'll be driving back from one of the last tournaments, and Aaron is suddenly going to realize that he missed the reunion at Grandma's, missed playing in the swimming pool with his cousins, and missed building a tree fort with his neighbors. I have no doubt that Aaron loves baseball and you love watching him play. But how will he feel about baseball at the end? And if you continue this pattern for the next eight years, that will be twenty-four thousand dollars just for Aaron. What about Jared, your younger son?"

Their faces softened a bit as they realized some of the peripheral implications of offering their son this opportunity.

And while I realize that "tree fort" logic isn't nearly as compelling as the promises and possibilities of elite sports, I do want families to weigh the actual costs of participation.

As you might imagine, as an athletics director, I have had a version of this conversation on more occasions than I can count. And invariably, when I suggest that a child might be missing out on something of equal or greater value, parents insist:

"Oh no, he loves it; he *loves* it!"

"It's hard, because our kids really enjoy it."

"She is begging me to do it."

While a lot of us would exercise much more caution about sinking our time and money into our children's other endeavors—travel abroad, pricey laptops, spring break at Myrtle Beach—when it comes to youth sports, we're often more willing to jump in first and ask questions later. We believe that we owe it to our kids, and we're reluctant to disappoint them.

Mark and Beth Bergman, though, had the courage to disappoint their son by letting him know that the pricey league wasn't a choice their family would be making. Though I suspect it was a tough conversation, they later shared with me that he cried for a short time and then never mentioned it again.

Whether or not we're able to articulate it, the decisions to pour money into our children's sporting experiences—which we identify as "investments"—are often made with the hope they will "pay off" with a college scholarship.

QUICK HISTORY LESSON

The first athletic competition between colleges or universities in the United States is thought to have been a highbrow crew regatta between Harvard and Yale in 1852. The two-mile race was held on Lake Winnipesaukee in New Hampshire. That was followed by the first baseball game between Amherst and Williams in 1859. Princeton and Rutgers are generally credited with playing the first intercollegiate football game in 1869.

Until the late 1800s, university athletics were student run. The incorporation of sports into the educational program of institutions of higher education, as well as high schools, was actually the idea of the great industrialists of the early 1900s. Folks like Andrew Carnegie and J. S. Rockefeller saw organized sport as a means to train, socialize, and control a workforce. They needed workers who were dependable, physically fit, team oriented, and obedient, and they believed that sports would develop those characteristics in young people.

However, when university presidents recognized the growing interest in sports activities—and the chance to make some money—they and their boards incorporated athletics into their education systems.

Athletic elitism was born.

Though we weren't around in the 1800s, we believe athletics began to spiral away from its origins of fun, health, socialization, and the development of character with the granting of scholarships based on athletic ability. Instead of valuing sports participation for those inherent merits, many people now play sports as a means to fame and fortune—namely, athletic superiority and college scholarships.

For about thirty years, nobody regulated the incentives for players to play on a college sports team. In 1906 the National Collegiate Athletic Association (NCAA) was formed to protect students "from the dangers and exploitative athletic practices of the time." But it was fifty years before the NCAA began attempts to regulate the scholarship concept, and those first attempts were futile; it took another twenty years until the NCAA set a limit on the number of football scholarships. In 1973 the NCAA split its membership into Divisions I, II and III, allowing Divisions I and II to offer athletic scholarships. Division III schools are not permitted to offer athletic scholarships and cannot include participation in sports in any criteria for awarding financial aid.

What exists today in American colleges and universities has very little to do with educational values. And it's not just at the Division I level; the integration of athletics and academics at the Division III level is also an ongoing struggle.

It is also peculiarly American. "The marriage of highly competitive, elite athletics and the educational system was a uniquely American experiment," writes John Gerdy in *Air Ball*. The high school and college sports scene in Canada is less intense than that of the United States. Canadian high school students seeking scholarships or professional careers look to enroll in a United States college or university. (The exception to this more laid-back Canadian rule is ice hockey. There are reports of eight- to ten-year-olds having ice hockey practices at five o'clock in the morning and travel teams of little kids traveling all over the province—and beyond—for competition.)

In most European countries, the sports teams in schools are largely intramural. The elite athletes participate in the local community club programs centered on geographic areas, so the teams represent their towns. The lack of competition for resources allows schools in Europe to develop programs consistent with the educational values of the classroom.

And in the case of soccer (*fútbol*), it must be better for athletics as well. European countries are the ones consistently winning the men's World Cup!

THE ONGOING TUG BETWEEN ATHLETICS AND ACADEMICS

As an educator, I (Dave) see the pull between school and sports every day in our schools. In the high school near my college campus, students miss class time to ride a bus two hours to a competition. Makeup games trump and bump band practice. Many more people attend basketball or soccer games than music concerts or theater productions. And the scores of games are published by the local media and put on websites, while academics get very little recognition. The athletic success of our children has now become part of the American dream that goes along with the four-bedroom house, good job, and two-car garage. Parents still talk about their dreams for their children in terms of "getting an education," but that dream may have more to do with the pride and prestige of athletic success.

The dance between athletics and education can be most unwieldy at the collegiate level.

The landscape changed forever when we began paying young people to do something they should be doing for the pure fun and joy of the experience. Universities may even begin to see student athletes in terms of how they benefit the institution rather than making sure that the institution benefits the student. The extrinsic value or reward of a college scholarship has replaced the intrinsic value of playing the game for its true meaning.

Athletes at Northwestern University are now actually considered *employees* of the university and therefore have the right to unionize. The landmark ruling by the National Labor Relations Board has sent shock waves through higher education. And while the NCAA disagreed with the ruling and continues to insist on identifying "student athletes" first as *students*, attorneys for the players prevailed by offering a different, and possibly more realistic, picture. They argued that college football, for all practical purposes, is a commercial enterprise that relies on players' labor to generate billions of dollars in revenue.

All of this was set in motion when the college athletic scholarship was established.

So to what degree are these athletes—"employed" by the university—students?

While many of the young people playing sports in college are capable of doing the academic work in college, far too many of them are not. Athletic scholarships are based on athletic ability, not academic merit. Some Division I institutions, where the majority of academic fraud cases are found, develop "crib" courses and "soft" majors. Universities spend millions on personal tutors who travel with the teams around the country—and, as with a recent case at the University of North Carolina–Chapel Hill, often do the work for athletes—all because of what these players can do for the school through athletics.

While these universities are giving their athletes some education, often it isn't anywhere close to the level of academic rigor expected of nonathletes. Often it isn't adequate preparation for a career in any field. Many elite college players never find satisfactory or successful employment after college. For them, college was not good preparation for life.

The philosophy of the athletics department at Eastern Mennonite University, the Division III school where I (Dave) work, is a little different. We recognize and accept that many of our student athletes are coming to us with their first priority being playing a sport. (I mean, we have spent more than a year recruiting them and trying to convince them to come!) We understand that those students are coming in through the "athletic window." But we become responsible for assisting them in their athletic and academic pursuits with the goal of making the college diploma the most important thing by the time they are seniors.

We believe that a lot of education happens outside the classroom, so we are committed to helping each student athlete learn from each of her experiences to prepare her for life after college. I have seen many young people change their perspective on the balance between athletics and academics; it is a most gratifying experience. As each one will be a person a lot longer than he or she will be an athlete, the change in perspective is necessary for success in life.

Let me also be clear that even though those of us at the Division III level cannot offer athletic scholarships, academics can easily become secondary to the athletic experience. Unfortunately, winning is the indicator of success, so coaches at all levels are spending hours watching AAU basketball tournaments, Junior Olympic volleyball classics, cup soccer tournaments, and baseball showcases. All of this is an effort to find the next young person who can help coaches develop or maintain a successful program, which will draw more students.

Some schools within Division III include leadership as criteria for financial aid and include athletic participation as a type of leadership. When my son Ryan was being recruited to a Division III school, he was offered a $15,000 presidential grant for leadership—even though his grades were average and he had no other leadership involvements at school other than sports. I don't think he was even captain of the basketball team! But he was six foot nine, and his high school basketball team had been successful in the state tournament.

EFFECTIVE?

You may be wondering, what does this have to do with my five-year-old?

We would argue *everything*.

The cost of a college education, coupled with the prestige of having children who are good athletes, causes many parents to get caught up in the dream of an athletic scholarship. And it has led adults to organize programs that "find the best and leave the rest."

So whether or not we explicitly state it, the college athletic scholarship has a huge impact on youth sports as we know them today.

As Division I collegiate programs got caught up in this notion—that elite athletic programs would support their educational values and help promote the university—they were, of course, recruiting and showcasing the very best talent.

That means that Division I programs have become farm systems for the professional programs. And high schools have become farm systems for the college programs. And youth sports have become a farm system for the high school varsity programs.

In *Air Ball*, John Gerdy observes that the experiment of mixing elite athletics with higher education has failed. But it remains the force behind the powerful impact that sports have had on culture and societal values. He writes, "The intensity of everything connected to the athletic experience, from recruiting, to individual commitment to the sport, to the level of play, has increased at every level, from peewee to professional leagues, all driven by the increasingly professionalized nature of the entire sports system."

Athletic scholarships shifted youth sports from opportunities for participation by the masses to a carefully organized system of identifying and training the elite athlete. All efforts are to find the best and leave the rest.

Although this may seem far removed from the Soccer Stars at Justin's daycare in chapter 1, it's a fact: *this* is the system that is shaping the athletic programs in your community. This is the system driving the anxiety that so many of us feel.

TEMPTATION FOR PARENTS TO "INVEST"

That being said, we realize that this historical unfolding isn't the palpable reality in which you live every day.

Today, your kid is just harassing you to play for a certain team that his friend is on. And as you fill out your child's birth-date on the online registration, you simply count the experience a win because your video game–addicted son will be outside, will get some exercise, and will play with his friends.

But as you enter your credit card information or write out the check, you notice yourself justifying the expense by rea-soning that it is an "investment." And since investments typi-cally, ideally, have some sort of return, the return you're hoping for—either consciously or, because of the way athletics have unfolded in our country, unconsciously—is the taste of a col-lege scholarship.

We can't state this strongly enough: the odds show that youth sports are one of the worst "investments" you'll ever make.

Mark Hyman, author of books on youth sports and an assistant professor at George Washington University, explains, "Parents think these investments are justified; they think it will lead to a full ride to college. That's highly misinformed. The percentage of high school kids who go on to play in college is extremely small. In most sports it's under 5 percent. And the number for kids get-ting school aid is even smaller—it's 3 percent."

In 2003–4, NCAA institutions gave athletic scholarships to about 2 percent of the 6.4 million athletes playing those sports in high school four years earlier. If your athlete was in the top 3 percent in her school, on an average-size squad it would mean that she was one of the best two or three players of her sport at the school in the last decade. And even if your superstar is in that slim minority that receives some aid, it is unlikely she'll receive a full ride.

"What I tell parents is if you want to get a scholarship for your kids, you're better off investing in a biology tutor than a quarterback coach," Hyman advises. "There's much more school dollars for academics."

The average college athletic scholarship, for the slim 3 percent of high school athletes who play in college, is about $10,000, but in sports like baseball or track and field, a student athlete can receive as little as $2,000. And the scholarship has to be awarded each year—which means that if a coach finds another player better than you, it is possible to have your scholarship reduced or taken away. If you're paying $40,000 for tuition, the athletic scholarship simply doesn't go very far.

One of my (Dave's) college buddies has a son who was on scholarship for baseball at a university in the Southeast. Between Dane's junior and senior year, the NCAA reduced the number of scholarships baseball programs were allowed to give out. (Yes, they can do that.) The coach informed Dane that he would be taking away part of his scholarship for his senior year and giving it to another player who was being more productive. I don't know if the injuries that Dane dealt with during his junior year influenced that decision. But he lost his athletic scholarship. Fortunately for Dane, he had good academic scholarships and was able to complete his college degree.

I agree with Hyman that families are much better off, financially, investing in their children's academics.

ADULT-DRIVEN MOTIVATION

We'd also like you to hear that this "investment" logic isn't coming from kids.

Kids start out playing sports because they're fun. Those who continue to play and excel are—hopefully!—doing it because they love it. It's parents—those of us who anticipate contributing toward college tuition and dreaming of college scholarship money—who are justifying "investments" in uniforms, gear, and registration fees.

Melissa Walsh, author of *The Rookie Hockey Mom*, agrees. She offers, "Ask any youth hockey player why he or she likes playing hockey. Not one will say, 'I like it cause I might get a scholarship.' Or, 'I like it cause I wanna miss all the fun social events during my teen years to play elite AAA hockey to be one of the less than one percent who make it into the NHL.'" No, kids play for fun. Too often adults—coaches and parents—are the ones making it into something other than that.

WHO GETS THE SCHOLARSHIPS?

Maybe you reason, "Someone is going to get those scholarships, so why not my kid?"

Professional athletes, and to a lesser degree the kinds of athletes who earn a full ride to college, are—and we mean this in the best possible way—*freaks of nature.*

They possess truly extraordinary physical capabilities—from the acuity of their vision to the agility of their bodies. Nearly every function in their body operates at a higher level, with greater efficiency, or with maximum output, depending on the sport and the skills needed to perform at high levels.

The women's basketball team at the college where I (Dave) work had the privilege of playing in the NCAA Division III basketball tournament for three consecutive years. During one of those appearances, the team played against a player who had received a full athletic scholarship to a Division I school, where she was named the Southeast Conference Freshman of the Year. Citing personal reasons—including wanting to have fun, not wanting basketball to feel like a job, and wanting to be appreciated for more than her basketball ability—she transferred to a Division III college near her home.

Watching her play was a great experience. Her physical attributes and basketball skills were far superior to those of the others on the floor. And some of those were simply impossible for any of her teammates to develop, even with ten thousand hours of practice. The neural messages being sent from her eyes to her brain and on to her arm muscles, telling her how hard to push the ball toward the basket based on the distance and angle she was from the basket: well, all these simply functioned at a much higher level than those of anyone else on the floor.

From my efforts to become a better golfer, I'm convinced that some people have a much greater capacity for muscle memory than I do. If I could only swing the club the same way each time, my success at getting that little ball into a little hole 350 yards away would be better. No doubt practice would help, but there may be a limit to my development of muscle memory. If athletic success was all about when we started playing or how often we played or how much we practiced, there would be a lot more of us playing at the highest levels. As one of my good friends told me, if you want your daughter to be an Olympian, you better check the genes.

Capability, however, is not enough. The athletes who succeed and continue to thrive in a sport and enjoy it aren't the ones who've been pushed through the ranks by their parents. They're the ones who are self-motivated to succeed. Intrinsic motivation, the love of the game, and the desire to get better and make your team better are ingredients for athletic success at any level.

Albert Zander, teaching and coaching at the high school level, observes, "The interesting thing in all this is that the athletes that actually get scholarships did not earn them because of special training. They all had the natural ability, talent, and self-motivation to succeed in sports. In other words, they could have picked multiple sports to succeed at because they were so gifted."

Clark Humphreys, associate head coach of the track program at Vanderbilt University, agrees that internal drive is what best serves young athletes who want to compete. "If there's an internal continued motivation," he offers, "if the kid has that, something they're striving toward, and maintains it, they have pretty good careers." He adds, "That internal drive, that is the key. That's when kids do well. Ya kinda gotta love it. If you don't, it'll be a hard, not fun, experience. Turns into more of a daily grind."

The American dream insists that anything is possible and that we can achieve anything we set our minds to. Not to be discouraging, but we have to tell you that in the case of athletics, that's simply not the case. There is a ceiling to the body's potential for improvement, and that ceiling is different for every child.

Even for the very best players, there are no guarantees of scholarship. There's a measure of chance involved.

Both of the boys in the Markham family were excellent soccer players and were actively involved in elite sports. Daniel played defense and his brother, Oliver, played offense.

Although Daniel was a much better player, the day a scout came to see the boys, Oliver happened to be the one to score two goals.

Guess who was offered the scholarship?

PHYSICAL LIMITS

Janice and Tom Scanlan adopted their daughter, Heidi, as an infant. She was their only child. They enrolled Heidi in a tumbling class at the age of two with the hopes of raising a champion gymnast.

The couple continued to spare no expense: private lessons, personal trainer, pricey equipment at home, the best coaches. They homeschooled Heidi so that they'd have the flexibility to move around the country to train with the best coaches in the best gyms, which they did. Not only did Heidi never miss a practice; at least one parent was always in attendance—offering her chalk for her hands, spraying water into her mouth, hovering constantly.

Heidi did have some natural ability, but all the money and personal trainers in the world could not make her a champion. By age fourteen, it was clear that Heidi would not make it to nationals. And yet last year was the Scanlans' thirteenth attempt to get her through the first stage of the U.S. qualifying competition. For the thirteenth year, Heidi didn't make the cut.

Heidi never went to a friend's birthday party. She never swam on a swim team or played a game of softball. She didn't have neighbors who knew her. She never went to a school dance. Today, at twenty-one, she's preparing for the next regional competition.

While Heidi certainly became an excellent gymnast, she hit a ceiling of what her body was capable of performing.

WHAT KINDS OF COSTS ARE WE TALKING ABOUT?

What makes parenting decisions particularly unwieldy is that you have no way of knowing whether your child will be a Heidi or a Michael Jordan.

Actually, Michael Jordan—who famously did not make his high school varsity basketball team as a sophomore because, at five foot eleven, he was deemed too short—is a great example. Because children develop at such varying rates, we may be quick to discount the child who hasn't fully developed by age ten or eleven.

Whether your young child is a Michael Jordan, a Heidi, or a Charlie Brown—and you likely can't know that without a crystal ball—it's important for every family to count the cost and weigh whether what they will "put in" will necessarily balance what their child or family will "get out."

Bob Bigelow, author of *Just Let the Kids Play*, was a first-round NBA draft pick in 1975. The first time Bigelow was on an organized basketball team was his freshman year in high school! So he's not convinced that sinking thousands of dollars into a young child's athletic experience is the ticket to success.

Bigelow recognizes the madness today in a variety of youth sports. "I live up here in ice hockey central," he says of Winchester, Massachusetts. "One of the hockey coaches up here told me there is no more cynical or delusional an adult than the parent of a sixteen-year-old kid who is pretty good but is not going to get a scholarship. The parents have spent all this money and they still have to pay for college."

Tina is a "volleyball mom." The club volleyball season begins the minute school leagues end in November and runs through March for regional teams and June or early July for national ones. In addition to tournaments, thirteen-year-olds practice twice a week, and practices increase with age.

When Tina's daughter began playing club volleyball in Washington as a seventh grader, her family paid $2,500 for her to participate on a regional team. This included tournament entry fees, food, hotel stays, and bus and air transportation. Uniforms were $350 extra. The costs for girls playing on regional and national teams came closer to $7,000.

And Tina *still* had to pay for college.

As the chair of the Department of Tourism, Recreation, and Sport Management at the University of Florida, Michael Sagas had a pretty good idea what to expect when his daughter started playing travel soccer. But even he was taken aback by the tally when her team started playing in regional and national tournaments.

Her latest season, which ended July 24, cost the family $18,115.41, Sagas said, adding, "It's ridiculous."

We don't know if the University of Florida has tuition breaks for the children of faculty. But chances are good that Sagas will still have to pay for college.

Hockey mom Melissa Walsh sees right through the "investment" language so many of us use to justify pouring a lot of cash into our kids' recreation. She notes, "Parents who think paying for youth hockey is an 'investment' toward their kid's college tuition or career stardom would be better off putting the money in the bank to accrue interest for a trust fund."

This is what we've been saying: bank it or pay for an academic tutor.

Spread the wealth

When your child does enjoy privileged athletic opportunities, consider "sponsoring" the cost of the opportunity for a child with fewer resources. This may also include identifying such a child and providing transportation. Leagues and camps may be open to welcoming, and even sponsoring, a child with fewer resources, but they may not have established social networks to reach out to these families.

A great way to serve kids is to partner with a local congregation in an under-resourced neighborhood. Does your congregation have a relationship with another church in your area or denomination? Connect with a pastor who can help to facilitate the relationship. Let that congregation be recognized as the child's sponsor, and keep your contribution private. You can take on the legwork to organize the child's registration, transportation, meals, and gear.

What we're really "buying" with the dollars we turn over on behalf of our athletic children, Walsh believes, isn't a ticket to an eventual scholarship lottery. Rather, she explains, "What a hockey parent buys her kid when submitting that ice payment is a fun, meaningful experience. There are also those priceless lessons in humility, work ethic, playing for [the] team, and honing will-to-win instincts."

Our hope is that parents can simply be more honest, like Walsh, about where their money is going. For the majority of parents and families, the money is not really going into a college investment fund. It's buying an experience for our children that we hope will be fun and meaningful.

Christian stewardship—how we're spending the money, time, and energy God has lent us—is at the heart of what it means to be a Christian parent. Perhaps even more than the words we teach our kids, our children are learning from our lives and the choices we make. They notice where we put our dollars. They see how we spend our time and whom we share it with. They recognize what takes up most of our energy.

Youth sports are one area, among many, where we have the opportunity to live out our own Christian stewardship in a way that forms our children and influences the world God loves. May God bless you as you purpose to pattern your life after Jesus for the children who are patterning their lives after you.

Q&A with Margot

Question: If we have the money, why wouldn't we spend it on our kids' sports?

Answer: One belief that has permeated popular Christian culture is that our lives ought to revolve around the members of our nuclear families. As parents, it's easy to convince ourselves that we're loving our kids well by giving them every opportunity: elite private schools; extravagant athletic, music, or academic opportunities; privileged summer camp experiences; even extravagant Christian mission trips!

And while it's important to care for our families, the Scriptures also challenge us to see and live beyond ourselves: loving our neighbors and caring for the poor. The way we use our resources is one of the ways we're called to love others the way we love ourselves. Sometimes those "others" will live under the same roof we do, and sometimes the "others" will be those who are radically different from us. In a kingdom economy, the ways we spend the money that God has entrusted to us matters deeply. It's what Jesus meant when he warned, "For where your treasure is, there your heart will be also" (Matthew 6:21).

As you make decisions about the athletic opportunities that are available to your children, know that how you spend your money matters.

The chart on the next page shows a few possibilities as you begin to think about spending, and not spending, from a kingdom perspective.

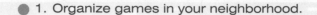 1. Organize games in your neighborhood.

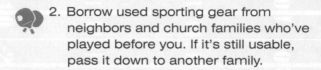 2. Borrow used sporting gear from neighbors and church families who've played before you. If it's still usable, pass it down to another family.

3. Encourage your child to play for his or her school team.

4. Choose to play in an affordable local league that includes kids with fewer resources.

5. Obtain used sporting gear online or at used sporting goods stores.

6. When your child plays on teams, such as school teams, with kids from families with various income ranges, discretely offer the coach money to cover some of the inevitable "extras" for kids from lower-income families: spirit T-shirts, warmup jackets, and so on.

7. Support athletic ministries, like Timoteo, that are providing opportunities for kids with fewer resources to develop physically, spiritually, and emotionally.

Conclusion

How Do We Talk to Our Kids about Sports?

My (Margot's) son Rollie, an eighth grader, was playing baseball for his middle school. The team had struggled the previous year, and in its second game of the season was up against the best team in the league.

I admit that I can become more invested in the drama of a competition than is helpful. So if there were ever a game for me to sit out, it would be this one.

When Rollie's dad texted to say the final score was 14–1, I knew I'd made the right choice. By the time Rollie got home, there was only time for homework and a shower before bedtime.

The next morning Rollie and I walked to school together.

"Hey, Rollie, sorry about that hard game yesterday against Lucas," I said.

"What?" Rollie asked. "What are you talking about? It was great."

I was confused. "Say more," I urged, curious.

"Well," Rollie explained, "we didn't get mercy-ruled. And we scored a run on them!"

The game I assumed had been a humiliating, soul-crushing defeat had actually been—from my son's perspective—a victory of which to be proud!

One of the best gifts we can give our children who are involved in sports is allowing them to narrate their own experience.

BEFORE PLAY AND DURING PLAY

How we narrate what happened during a game is the kind of conversation that happens at the back end of our kids' experience of sports. At the front end, we encourage you to engage your children in a conversation about what it is that they value and the degree to which they want to be involved.

For a lot of us, that conversation requires a lot of humility. It means that we're not pushing our agenda—or our unfulfilled dreams!—onto our kids.

One baseball commissioner in Ohio has seen the fallout when these conversations don't happen.

ONE BASEBALL COMMISSIONER

Veronica is a friend of ours who lives in Iowa. She described to us a Little League commissioner—we'll call him Chuck—who lives and breathes youth baseball. She insists, "He loves, loves, loves it."

But Chuck and some other dads have gotten fed up with the travel team phenomenon that takes kids away from their local communities and insists on early specialization. Veronica found this post, from Chuck, on a Facebook group for their local rec league:

> Last night a few kids who are playing travel baseball were telling me about their teams and schedules. When they mentioned tournaments the weekend of April 11th, I said it's too bad that they were going to miss our Opening Day. They had no idea and immediately expressed disappointment. I really felt bad for them as I could see their disappointment on their faces. These kids love playing with their school friends and, in the case of our organization, know what a special Opening Day we have.
>
> But it made me think: How many parents actually discuss with their kids the travel tournament schedules before committing their kids to play in them? I know many of these kids understandably love playing with their travel teams and I do not in any way discourage the same. But, I have to wonder how many of these kids are making these choices versus their parents making these choices for them?
>
> Maybe a little dialogue between the parents and kids would help the parents keep their kids' travel coaches better informed. TALK to your kids and let them make informed decisions. They may choose to play in the tournaments that weekend. Based on the disappointment expressed by the kids last night, I know a few who'd rather stay home

So often it's just more expedient to make a decision for our children—to play or not to play—rather than engaging them in the process. That conversation, though, is a great opportunity to help your child think through his or her choices as you communicate the kinds of values that you mean to instill. You can find conversation starters in this chapter.

WHOSE EVENT?

Deciding whether to play is just the first conversation, among many, in which you have the opportunity to communicate to your child that his or her experience matters to you.

Think about what happens after the whole family has watched the Friday night high school football game or Saturday morning peewee soccer game. We pile into the minivan and we *debrief* it.

"Does that coach know anything about the game?!"

"Why was she playing your position?"

"That ref was the worst!"

"Next year I'm gonna get you on a different team."

We're not talking about sixteen-year-olds. We're talking about six-year-olds!

Worst questions to discuss on the way home from the game

1. Who won? Why didn't you win?

2. Did you score? Why didn't you score?

3. Why were your teammates so bad?

4. Why didn't the coach play you more?

5. What was wrong with the ref?

Six-year-old Sam doesn't care about any of that. He's already thinking about what flavor of ice cream he'll get on the way home. Or he's laughing because Will had two different color socks on. That's where Sam's head is.

But too often we, as parents, hijack the event and make it our own.

When we get in the van and start doing our own ESPN SportsCenter analysis of the game, we rob our children of reflecting on it themselves. The beauty of the experience for children is to understand what's going on. But when we tell them what's going on, we rob our children by making it all about us.

Changing the Game Project founder John O'Sullivan, who notes that ref-slugging parents really are few and far between, is concerned about this tendency. "What is far more destructive when it comes to youth sports," O'Sullivan insists, "are parents who use the car ride home to criticize and critique their kids, at a moment when the kids just want to unwind after the game."

Not only do we "critique" but we also convince ourselves that doing so is exactly what makes us good parents.

We tell ourselves that we're "engaging" with our kids.

We rationalize that we care about what they care about.

We reason that we're "helping them" improve.

In the end, though—and maybe with the best of intentions—when we impose our own opinions by second-guessing the ref's calls, the coaches' strategies, or even an opponent's play, we make the game about us.

THE RIDE HOME AFTER THE GAME

When John O'Sullivan asked kids leaving a league what their least favorite moment in sports was, he was saddened by the answer he heard too often: the ride home after the game.

Eight best questions to discuss on the way home from the game

1. How did the game go?
2. Did you have a good time today?
3. Did you learn anything today?
4. What was the best part of the experience for you?
5. What do you think will happen in practice this week?
6. Did anything happen that made you feel bad?
7. What do you think the team needs to do to improve?
8. What did you notice a friend doing that helped the team?

Tip: Don't evaluate. Talk about anything other than results!

O'Sullivan observes, "Emotions are high, disappointment, frustration and exhaustion are heightened for both player and parent, yet many parents choose this moment to confront their child about a play, criticize them for having a poor game, and chastise their child, their teammates, their coach, and their opponents." O'Sullivan adds, "There could not be a less teachable moment in your child's sporting life than the ride home, yet it is often the moment that well-intentioned parents decide to do all their teaching."

CONVERSATIONS AFTER THE SEASON IS OVER

When my (Margot's) daughter, Zoe, had a particularly rough season in a sport, she vowed she would not play that sport the next season. In my opinion, there would be some good reasons not to play and some good reasons to play. I also knew that by the time the next season rolled around, we both would probably have forgotten most of them!

We encourage you to have a conversation at the end of each season to help your child debrief and reflect on his or her experience. It might be as simple as a game of "best and worst": What were the best parts of playing? What were the worst parts of playing? Or if there were particular issues that concerned you, you might steer the conversation to cover those.

Coach Clark Humphreys, dad to two children under age ten and associate head coach of the track program at Vanderbilt University, values a child finishing up a season, even when it's difficult. When it's over, though, he advises, "Let kids direct. Not quit. Then have the conversation after the season, if you don't want to do it next [season]. Offer the options."

Questions to help a child unpack his or her experience at the end of a season

1. What were the best things about playing? What did you most enjoy?

2. What were the worst things about playing? What did you not enjoy?

3. What makes you look forward to playing again next year?

4. What makes you think you might not want to play next year?

Even better than the eight questions on the way home from the game

Let your child set the tone and choose the agenda for the car ride home. She might just want to sip her juice box. He might want to eat Doritos. She might want to tell you how silly it was that Sebastian was making funny faces during halftime. He might want to tell you that his coach is going to have knee surgery.

Tip: Pay attention to your child and his or her experience.

HOW TO DISCUSS WHETHER TO PLAY

Whenever an opportunity to play comes along, give your child a voice in the decision-making process. One of the most helpful things you can do as a parent is to help your child see the big-picture consequences of a decision.

Here's a menu of topics* you might discuss with your child:

1. Do you want to play this sport? On a scale of one to ten, one being "not really" and ten being "more than anything," how much do you want to play? (Watch your child's face. Listen to the tone of her voice. You know your child: Is she sincere, or just saying what she thinks you want to hear? Do you notice any hesitation?)

2. Do you want to seize this particular opportunity to play this sport?

3. Are there other ways you could play this sport? (If possible, mention opportunities that are more rigorous and less rigorous.)

4. Here's the kind of coaching style you might expect. (Or: We're not sure what coaching style you can expect.)

5. These are the friends you might know or meet if you play.

6. These are the friends you might not see as frequently if you play.

7. Here's what the season will look like: Practices will be this often, this long, and this rigorous. Games will be this frequent and this long. Travel time will look like this. Expectations of you, outside of games and practices, include this.

8. Here's what you could be sacrificing to play. (Involvement in other sports, family functions, invitations from friends, and so on.)

9. How much free time do you need or want in your schedule? (This might be hard for your child to answer, but you know how he or she is wired. Note relevant instances from your child's experience where you've observed his or her need, or lack thereof, for unscheduled time.)

10. What classes are you taking this year that might require a lot of homework time? If you play, do you anticipate being able to balance your academic load?

11. Here's what you'll gain by playing.

12. Here are the risks, physical and emotional.

13. Here's the financial cost for our family.

14. Here's the investment of time this means for our family.

15. Up until now, these are the ways I've seen you thrive and grow and develop as a result of your involvement with this sport.

16. Up until now, these are the ways I've seen you struggle and wrestle and wither as a result of your involvement with this sport.

*Not all of these discussion points will be appropriate for every child at every age. Pick and choose those that seem most relevant for your situation.

Closing note from Dave

I am not anti-sport.

I've simply wanted to paint a realistic picture of our sports culture as a starting point for reframing our perspective. I am deeply committed to sports and the value of athletics to enhance an educational experience, provide a place to meet God, and develop quality characteristics and skills that will last a lifetime. The sports field or arena should be a learning laboratory for the wholesome development of young people.

But over the last few decades we have lost that vision and have used sports as a means to gain fame, fortune, value, and worth for our children, our families, our schools, and our communities. We've bought in without counting the cost. We've also bought into the myths without knowing the facts.

Today it is our responsibility to challenge, encourage, and support our families to stand in the face of the current winds and find alternatives that will benefit children more than today's programs.

I'd love to hear from you, so let's continue the conversation. Email me at overplayed.king@gmail.com with your thoughts.

For the sake of the great kids we know and love,

—Dave

Closing note from Margot

As builders of God's kingdom, I'm excited that you've had this chance to pause and consider the daily choices your family is making about youth sports. I want to challenge you—in the bleachers, on the sidelines, in the minivan—to live out the values you hold.

Your kids are watching.

Do they see you loving God and others by befriending a family on the sidelines who doesn't speak English?

Do they notice that when parents have to send in fees for uniforms, you slip the coach a donation to use at her discretion for a family in need?

Do they recognize the ways you're living a vibrant life of love for others, in response to Jesus Christ, after you drop them at practice?

I'm convinced that as you live out your calling as a bearer of salt and light in the world, your kids will learn, in their deep places, what it means to belong to Jesus.

Bless you and your family as you are transformed more and more into the image of Christ.

For the sake of the kingdom Jesus ushered in,

—Margot

Bonus Tips and Resources

for Coaches, Churches, and Parents

I f you'd like children in your area—your home, your school, your church, or your community—to have a different experience of sports, you can make that happen.

If you're a parent, you can choose leagues that reflect your values. You can encourage your child and help him or her process and understand his or her experience. You can gather a few other families to create a team that meets the needs of your child.

If you're a coach, you can give players a great experience to learn and to grow. You can avoid practice schedules that overtax families. You can give kids the opportunity to play a variety of positions.

If you're a church with appropriate facilities, you might begin a league that offers families a healthy and life-giving option for their kids.

Here are a few ideas to get your own creative juices flowing.

FIVE IDEAS FOR COACHES

1. Have every kid play every position, including the bench.

2. Offer parents permission to skip several games.

3. Ask that parents not attend practices unless they're helping you coach the team.

4. Ban scoreboards when you're able.

5. Let fun and learning be your prime directives.

FIVE IDEAS FOR CHURCHES

1. Avoid going to battle

Don't make the battle between elite sports and the middle school youth group. You won't win. The conflict isn't between a weekend tournament and a church service project weekend. It's not a battle between Wednesday evening youth Bible study and varsity wrestling practice. And it's not a war between sports and Christians demanding no sports on Sunday or people of other faiths making time for their own religious observances.

The current youth sports scene confronts families with tough decisions, and pastors and youth leaders must seek to understand that. Families will be best served as they're equipped to evaluate the larger picture and asked to identify what's important to them. But that requires a gentle spirit rather than a judgmental one.

2. Engage the conversation

When we speak at churches and organizations, parents express such relief that someone is at last addressing their concerns! Consider hosting a workshop during the Sunday school hour or on a weekday evening. Find our useful guide at www.heraldpress.com/overplayed.

3. Support coaches

Most coaches give their time generously, and many of them see their coaching as a way that they live out their faith in their community. Some of these coaches are probably in your congregation. Thank them for caring for kids, share this book, and open up a conversation!

4. Offer alternatives

If resources are available—space, coaches, and so on—run alternate programs through your church. This is also a great opportunity to invite kids from the neighborhood to participate.

5. Encourage pastors to engage

When a pastor or volunteer who works with church youth attends a child's game, it communicates to a family—and to other families in the bleachers—that a child matters. Though admittedly unwieldy in larger churches, joining families where they spend their time is a great way to nurture folks in your congregation.

FIVE CREATIVE SOLUTIONS FOR PARENTS

1. Facilitate free play

Drive around to the homes of your child's friends and gather them up as you might for practice. Then release them at a public park, or in your backyard, with a playground ball. Set them loose and see what happens!

2. Support traditional local leagues

The Changing the Game Project is educating towns to elimi-nate travel teams and bring everybody back in-house. Then, as in days of old, all-star teams can play in local tournaments. Support youth sports programs that eliminate selection of elite teams until at least age twelve.

3. Support leagues that are committed to your values

If your area has leagues that are designed for fun and learning skills, choose these over more competitive leagues. Find leagues that value fun, safe, character-building competition.

4. Create alternative teams

If you have the freedom to do it, gather a team of players and arrange games between other local teams. One couple found seven other families who were also frustrated with what was available, and they created their own travel team. They chose to play in only three tournaments and had a great experience.

5. Create alternative leagues

Create a novel new league with other families with similar con-cerns. Games could be played at the same site on the same day (every other week, for example). You could begin the event with a picnic or have a dessert party after each game. Don't keep records, and maybe even mix up the players on the teams. Sponsor a coed parent game as part of the festivities.

FIVE TIPS FOR FAMILIES WHO CHOOSE ELITE SPORTS

1. Honor designated commitments outside of sports

At the beginning of the season, look at your family calendar to identify conflicts. When sports conflict with vacation, family celebrations, church activities, or a best friend's birthday, decide together which commitments outside of sports you will honor. Let the coach know ahead of time which practices or games your child will not be able to attend because of these other commitments.

2. Be purposeful about the values you're developing

Discuss with your child what values he or she will be developing through this experience. Perhaps your child will commit to befriending an unpopular child on the team. Maybe she'll decide that whenever she's on the bench she'll be the servant who offers water during time-outs to players on the field. He might use some of his allowance to help offset costs of gear for a player with fewer resources. Be purposeful about the character your child is developing. Your purpose has to be larger than athletic performance, the chance to play on the "best" teams, or your child's individual statistics.

3. Invest in relationships

One temptation a family may face is making the experience all about the child. Let your child know that other players, their families, coaches, referees, and even their own siblings matter. Learn the names of every child on the team. Share a sports drink with the refs at halftime. Offer to watch the coach's toddler. Help your child see her involvement as an opportunity to invest in others. Cheer for every player. Offer to carpool to tournaments and practices.

4. Honor your other children

Travel teams and elite sports typically require a hefty investment of time. While time spent with a team can be valuable to your athlete, it's not always so valuable to the children who are forced to tag along. Find creative solutions for these children. If driving home during practice isn't feasible, spend time reading with a little one in the bleachers. During a tournament weekend, plan a special visit for your littlest one with Grandma. As parents, we do the best we can. Do your best to honor the needs of your other children.

5. Help your child process his or her experience

Without help from a trusted adult, it would be natural for a child to make assumptions that may or may not be true: "Because my parents have invested this time and money, I need to perform for them" or "If I'm not a starter, if I don't score, if I don't excel, I have failed." You give your child a great gift as you help her process her experience as an athlete.

ADVICE FROM ONE ELITE-SPORT MOM WHOSE CHILD SPECIALIZED IN ONE SPORT

Specializing in one sport early isn't for everyone, as we've said in these pages. For families who do make that choice, however, here is one mom's advice.

1. Do your own thing

Don't "team hop" or "coach hop," bouncing around to find the best. And also don't be afraid to choose a different program from the one that "everyone else" thinks is the best. Get the best advice, not the mob's advice.

2. Help your child set wise goals

Encourage your child to set intermediate and attainable goals, and then set new ones once those are met. Don't be that idiot Olympics-or-bust parent, because then you'll think it's all for nothing if your kid doesn't get there. Instead, be happy and amazed by the ride and where your child does go. Goal setting is a good habit for life!

3. Be the quietest parent on the team

You give your child a gift when you let the coach do the coaching.

4. Be gracious

Be gracious to those who compliment your child, and simply disengage from those who have unkind things to say.

5. Encourage well-roundedness

Really work on your child's well-roundedness. Do not make that sport the only thing you talk about. In fact, concentrate on talking about absolutely anything else at home.

6. Disengage from the "crazies"

(Those are her words, not ours.) Yes, there are parents who push their kids too hard to excel. It's likely you'll enjoy your experience more if you create a bit of distance from the rushing river of madness.

7. Avoid drama

Drama is your worst enemy, and your child's. Don't start it, and stay away from it.

8. Listen

Listen to your young person. Is she driving the agenda to specialize year-round, or are you? Is he satisfied to enjoy his current level of sport and not make it to the Olympics? Keep the conversation with your child open during each new season.

MARKS OF A LEAGUE THAT DOES IT DIFFERENTLY

Are you up for organizing a casual league where kids can learn and have fun? Here are some ideas to consider and to stimulate your own.

- Purpose to teach skills.

- Eliminate the scoreboard.

- Commit to every child playing every position—including sitting on the bench and coaching third base!

- Mix up teams every week: boys versus girls, tall versus short, odd-numbered birthdays versus even, and so on.

- Change the size of the field; cut it in half.

- Set up four goals instead of two to challenge kids to think creatively.

- Exclude parents from practices.

- Institute "Silent Saturdays," when parents are permitted to attend but no one is allowed to talk—including the coach!

RESOURCES FOR FAMILIES WHO WANT TO DO SPORTS DIFFERENTLY

Websites
Changing the Game Project
http://changingthegameproject.com

The Aspen Institute's Project Play
http://www.aspenprojectplay.org/the-facts

Catch 22 Foundation
http://catch22foundation.com

National Alliance for Youth Sports
www.nays.org

HEADS UP to Youth Sports
www.cdc.gov/headsup/youthsports

John Gerdy
www.johngerdy.com

Books

Andrews, James R. *Any Given Monday: Sports Injuries and How to Prevent Them, For Athletes, Parents, and Coaches—Based on My Life in Sports Medicine.* New York: Scribner, 2014.

Bigelow, Bob, Tom Moroney, and Linda Hall. *Just Let the Kids Play: How to Stop Other Adults from Ruining Your Child's Fun and Success in Youth Sports.* Deerfield Beach, FL: Health Communications, 2001.

Doyle, Dan, with Deborah Doermann Burch. *The Encyclopedia of Sports Parenting: Everything You Need to Guide Your Young Athlete.* New York: Skyhorse Publishing, 2013.

Farrey, Tom. *Game On: The All-American Race to Make Champions of Our Children.* New York: ESPN Books, 2008.

Hyman, Mark. *The Most Expensive Game in Town: The Rising Cost of Youth Sports and the Toll on Today's Families*. Boston: Beacon Press, 2012.

Hyman, Mark. *Until It Hurts: America's Obsession with Youth Sports and How It Harms Our Kids*. Boston: Beacon Press, 2009.

Matheny, Mike, and Jerry B. Jenkins. *The Matheny Manifesto: A Young Manager's Old-School Views on Success in Sports and Life*. New York: Crown Archetype, 2015.

O'Sullivan, John. *Changing the Game: The Parent's Guide to Raising Happy, High-Performing Athletes and Giving Youth Sports Back to Our Kids*. New York: Morgan James Publishing, 2014.

Notes

Introduction

page 12 Only 57 percent of families: "Importance of Family Dinner VIII," National Center on Addiction and Substance Abuse (CASA) at Columbia University, September 2012, http://www.casacolumbia.org/addiction-research/reports/importance-of-family-dinners-2012.

page 13 "I believe that . . . loud cheering": Mike Matheny, *The Matheny Manifesto: A Young Manager's Old-School Views on Success in Sports and Life* (New York: Crown, 2015), 15.

page 14 *Love one another*: John 13:34; paraphrase of Luke 2:52; Mark 10:43-44.

page 19 The Women's Sports Foundation reports: "Benefits: Why Sports Participation for Girls and Women," http://www.womenssportsfoundation.org/home/advocate/foundation -positions/mental-and-physical-health/benefits_why_sports_participation_for_girls_and_women.

Myth One

page 21 When Jennifer's son, Justin, was two years old: Names and identifying information of some of the people in this book have been changed.

page 24 The number of children between the ages: Bruce Kelley and Carl Carchia, "Hey, Data Data—Swing!" ESPN, July 16, 2013, http://espn.go.com/espn/story/_/id/9469252/hidden -demographics-youth-sports-espn-magazine.

page 24   "extreme, early focus on one sport": "What Does the Science Say about Athletic Development in Children?" *Aspen Institute's Project Play Research Brief*, September 2013, http://www.aspeninstitute.org/sites/default/files/content/docs/pubs/Project-play-september-2013-roundtable-resarch-brief.pdf.

page 27   He calculates that some families: Paul Sullivan, "The Rising Costs of Youth Sports, in Money and Emotion," *New York Times*, January 16, 2015, http://www.nytimes.com/2015/01/17/your-money/rising-costs-of-youth-sports.html?_r=0.

page 27   During his daughter's most recent season: Kelley Holland, "Shut Out: Young Athletes Sidelined by Money," CNBC, July 25, 2014, http://www.cnbc.com/id/101860953.

page 27   One out of five disadvantaged households: "Paying to Play: The High Cost of Youth Sports," FlipGive, June 9, 2014, http://blog.flipgive.com/paying-to-play-youth-sports.

page 28   "are participating with a vengeance": Kelley Holland, "European Vacation? Nah, Junior's Got a Soccer Tourney," *Today Parents*, July 23, 2014, http://www.today.com/parents/families-trading-summer-vacations-youth-sports-travel-1D79964589.

page 29   In 2014, 1.35 million children: Michelle Healy, "1.35 Million Youths a Year Have Serious Sports Injuries," *USA Today*, August 6, 2013, http://www.usatoday.com/story/news/nation/2013/08/06/injuries-athletes-kids-sports/2612429.

page 29   One in every five kids: Ibid.

page 29   Nearly half of all injuries: "Youth Sports Injuries Statistics," Stop Sports Injuries, http://www.stopsportsinjuries.org/media/statistics.aspx.

page 30   In fact, during the past thirty years: "Childhood Obesity Facts," Centers for Disease Control and Prevention, April 24, 2015, http://www.cdc.gov/HealthyYouth/obesity/facts.htm.

page 30   This included feeling undermined: "The Experiences of Children Participating in Organised Sport in the UK," National Society for the Prevention of Cruelty to Children, May 1, 2011, https://thecpsu.org.uk/resource-library/2013/the-experiences-of-children-participating-in-organised-sport-in-the-uk.

page 32 "There is absolutely no correlation": Bob Bigelow, "Is Your Child Too Young for Youth Sports or Is Your Adult Too Old?" in *Sports in School: The Future of an Institution*, ed. John Gerdy (New York: Teachers College, 2000), 10.

Myth Two

page 58 "Over four years of testing": David Epstein, *The Sports Gene: Inside the Science of Extraordinary Athletic Performance* (New York: Current, 2014), 40.

page 60 In response to the increased number: Arash Markazi, "Kobe: Europe's Players More Skillful," ESPN, January 3, 2015, http://espn.go.com/nba/story/_/id/12114523/kobe -bryant-says-european-players-more-skilled-americans -blames-aau.

Myth Three

page 83 Today the success rate: Eric Rosenhek, "The Gory Details of Tommy John Surgery," *The Good Point* (blog), July 1, 2009, http://thegoodpoint.com/tommy-john-surgery-procedure.

page 84 "There was a tenfold increase": Laken Litman, "Youth Pitchers Feeling the Pinch of Tommy John Surgery Epidemic," *USA Today*, July 23, 2014, http://ftw.usatoday .com/2014/07/tommy-john-surgery-youth-sports.

page 84 And unfortunately, these kids don't weather: Ibid.

page 84 "Children are pigeonholed into one sport": James R. Andrews with Don Yaeger, *Any Given Monday: Sports Injuries and How to Prevent Them for Athletes, Parents, and Coaches—Based on My Life in Sports Medicine* (New York: Scribner, 2014), 5.

page 85 "Left to themselves, children engaged": Lindsey Barton Straus, "Overuse Injuries and Burnout in Youth Sports: What We Know and What We Don't," MomsTeam.com, March 8, 2014, http://www.momsteam.com/health-safety/overuse-injuries- burnout-in-youth-sports-what-we-know-what-we-dont.

page 85 The *Clinical Journal of Sport Medicine* reports: William O. Roberts, "Overuse Injuries and Burnout in Youth Sports," *Clinical Journal of Sport Medicine* 24, no. 1 (2014): 1–2.

page 85   A recent study shows that high school athletes: Straus, "Overuse Injuries."

page 85   When Atlanta Braves pitcher John Smoltz: Nick Schwartz, "John Smoltz Warns Young Players About Tommy John Surgery in Hall of Fame Acceptance Speech," *USA Today*, July 26, 2015, http://ftw.usatoday.com/2015/07/john -smoltz-warns-young-players-about-tommy-john-surgery -in-hall-of-fame-acceptance-speech.

page 85   "I want to encourage": Nick Schwartz, "John Smoltz Warns Young Players about Tommy John Surgery in Hall of Fame Acceptance Speech," *For the Win*, July 26, 2015, http://ftw .usatoday.com/2015/07/john-smoltz-warns-young-players -about-tommy-john-surgery-in-hall-of-fame-acceptance -speech.

page 93   "You gotta get the money out": "Great Thoughts from Mark Messier and Mike Richter," Vimeo video, 5:03, posted by Thousand Islands Youth Hockey, https://vimeo.com/ 30793996.

Myth Four

page 103   "You just want to give your kids the best": Kelley Holland, "Costs for Youth Sports Set to Spiral . . . Again," CNBC, August 26, 2014, http://www.cnbc.com/id/101929871.

page 103   "It starts out that parents want their kids": Ibid.

page 116   "These trophies will be given back": David Mack, "An NFL Player Is Returning His Sons' Participation Trophies to Teach Them a Lesson," Buzzfeed, August 16, 2015, http:// www.buzzfeed.com/davidmack/this-nfl-star-sent-back -his-sons-participation-trophies#.caMJGXwW.

page 117   One poll reveals: Brooke De Lench, "Fun Is Still Number One Reason Kids Play Sports," MomsTeam.com, August 6, 2010, http://www.momsteam.com/successful-parenting/ fun-still-number-one-reason-kids-play-sports.

Myth Five

page 131-132   "Travel ball is not new": David Mendell, "Stealing Home: How Travel Teams Are Eroding Community Baseball," *Washington Post*, May 23, 2014, http://www.washingtonpost.com/opinions/stealing-home-how-travel-teams-are-eroding-community-baseball/2014/05/23/5af95d34-df6e-11e3-9743-bb9b59cde7b9_story.html.

page 140   In fact, research shows that children: Bruce Kelley and Carl Carchia, "Hey, Data Data—Swing!" ESPN, July 16, 2013, http://espn.go.com/espn/story/_/id/9469252/hidden-demographics-youth-sports-espn-magazine.

page 149   This ministry shines as one of the brightest examples: Learn more at www.timoteofootball.com.

Myth Six

page 166   According to a recent study, parents who overvalue: Eddie Brummelman et al., "Origins of Narcissism in Children," *PNAS Early Edition,* February 12, 2015, http://i2.cdn.turner.com/cnn/2015/images/03/09/narcissistic-parenting-study.pdf.

page 167   "Young children are young, impressionable": Christopher Andersonn with Barbara Andersonn, *Will You Still Love Me If I Don't Win? A Guide for Parents of Young Athletes* (New York: Taylor Trade Publishing, 2000), 8.

page 171   "The best situation for all of us": To read the letter in its entirety, go to www.mikematheny.com and click on "The Manifesto." Find more great reflections from Mike Matheny in *The Matheny Manifesto: A Young Manager's Old-School Views on Success in Sports and Life* (New York: Crown, 2015).

page 172   A recent mutation of the helicopter parent: "Here Come the Lawnmower Parents," *Inquisitr,* October 12, 2014, http://www.inquisitr.com/1535202/here-come-the-lawnmower-parents-a-breed-that-is-more-aggressive-than-helicopter-parents.

Myth Seven

page 184 "from the dangers and exploitative athletic practices":
Gerald D. Higginbotham, "Free Play," *Student Pulse* 3, no. 7
(2011), http://www.studentpulse.com/articles/552/2/free
-play-unmasking-and-ending-the-exploitation-of-ncaa
-student-athletes.

page 185 "The marriage of highly competitive": John Gerdy, *Air Ball:
American Education's Failed Experiment with Elite Athletics*
(Jackson: University Press of Mississippi, 2006), 13.

page 186 The landmark ruling by the National Labor Relations
Board: Brian Bennett, "Northwestern Players Get Union
Vote," ESPN, March 27, 2014, http://espn.go.com/college
-football/story/_/id/10677763/northwestern-wildcats
-football-players-win-bid-unionize.

page 189 "The intensity of everything connected": Gerdy, *Air Ball*, 23.

page 190 "Parents think these investments are justified": Paul
Sullivan, "The Rising Costs of Youth Sports, in Money and
Emotion," *New York Times*, January 16, 2015, http://www
.nytimes.com/2015/01/17/your-money/rising-costs-of
-youth-sports.html?_r=0.

page 191 "What I tell parents is if you want": Ibid.

page 197 Her latest season, which ended July 24: Kelley Holland,
"Shut Out: Young Athletes Sidelined by Money," CNBC,
July 25, 2014, http://www.cnbc.com/id/101860953.

page 198 "What a hockey parent buys her kid": Melissa Walsh, "Beer
League, Prospects," *The Rookie Hockey Mom* (blog), May
15, 2014, http://rookiehockeymom.com/1/post/2014/05/
beer-league-prospects.html.

Bonus Tips and Resources for Coaches, Churches, and Parents

page 205 When John O'Sullivan asked kids: John O'Sullivan,
"The Ride Home," Changing the Game Project, http://
changingthegameproject.com/the-ride-home-after-the-game.

The Authors

David King is director of athletics and associate director of development at Eastern Mennonite University in Harrisonburg, Virginia. He holds a ministerial license in Virginia Mennonite Conference for itinerant speaking on faith and athletics and has given presentations and sermons on the topic at churches, denominational assemblies, and conferences. King has taught and coached and was an administrator at the elementary, middle, and high school levels. Dave and his wife, Deb, have three adult children and two grandchildren.

Margot Starbuck is the author of six books, including the award-winning *Girl in the Orange Dress*. She is a widely sought-after speaker and columnist at *Today's Christian Woman* and an editorial advisor for *Gifted for Leadership*. A graduate of Westmont College and Princeton Seminary, Starbuck is the mother of three children and lives in Durham, North Carolina.